THE LEARNING CENTRE
HAMMERSMITH AND WEST
LONDON COLLEGE
GLIDDON ROAD
LONDON W14 9BL

0181 741 1688

Hammersmith and West London College

324385

SUGAR ROSES

—*for Cakes*—

SUGAR ROSES

for Cakes

TOMBI PECK

ALAN DUNN

TONY WARREN

CONTENTS

Introduction 6

TRADITIONAL ROSES 8

Wild At Heart 10
Dog Rose 12

Medieval Harvest Medley 16
Rosa Rugosa Hips 18
Purple Appleberries 19

Golden Days 20
'Golden Wings' 22

White Christmas *(Arrangement)* 26
'Boule de neige' 28
White Poplar 31
Miltonia Flavescens 32
Snowberries 34

Danish Romance 36
'Queen of Denmark' 38

Little Mermaid Spray 40

CLIMBER AND RAMBLER ROSES 42

Pink Perfection 44
'Mme. Cécile Brünner' 46

Blue Peter Rose Cake 48
'Blue Peter' 50

The Pompom Cake 52
'Old Blush' 54
'Cathedral Splendour' 57

MODERN ROSES 60

Favourite Ruby Wedding 62
'Pink Favourite' 64
Sea Holly 66
Mahonia Berries, 68
Eucalyptus Leaves 69

Diamond Jubilee 70
'Diamond Jubilee' 74
Ivy 77

324385

Painter Rose Displays 78
'Painter' 80

Susan's Wedding Cake 84
'Delilah' 86
Tradescantia 88
Arum Lily 89

Summer Solstice 90
'Chicago' 92
Dog's-Tooth Violet 94
Ruscus 96

Corsages 97

Pero's Pearl Cake 98

Quilted Box Cake 100
'Pascali' 103

'Elegance' 104

A Basket of Roses 106

Flamenco Hand-Tied Bouquet 108
'Breath of Life' 110
Vine Leaves 113
Blood Lilies 114

Starfish and Coral 116
'Peppermint' (Quick Rose) 118
Beetleweed and Bear Grass 121

Contemporary Arrangements 122

Winter Wedding *(Arrangement)* 124
'Massai' 126
Oriental Climbing Bittersweet 128

Handel's Messiah *(Spray)* 130
Gymea lily 132
White Watsonia 134
White Ginger 135

White Rose and Orchid Bridal Bouquet 136
'Canary Creeper' 138
Phragmipedium Orchid 140
Crocosmia Berries 143
Coelogyne Ochracea 144

Equipment and Techniques 145
Templates 150
Index 158
Acknowledgements 159
Suppliers 160

Introduction

Fossilized rose leaves have been found in North America, parts of Western and Central Europe and Japan. These date back some 4,000,000 years, predating mankind. Roses growing in China became popular as early as 500BC.

In Greek and Roman mythology, Aphrodite (Venus) the goddess of love, as illustrated in Botticelli's 'Birth of Venus', is said to have emerged from sea foam. Where the foam touched the land, white roses grew. Mythology indicates that her priestesses were clad in wreaths of white roses, and their paths strewn with them. This is still practised during some wedding ceremonies where rose petals are scattered in front of the bride. In another story Aphrodite, running to the assistance of her wounded lover, Adonis, is said to have caught herself on the thorns of a white rose, and where her blood fell on the rose they became red. This is also said to reflect the duality of the nature of love, with the white rose representing purity and innocence and the red rose representing desire and sexual gratification.

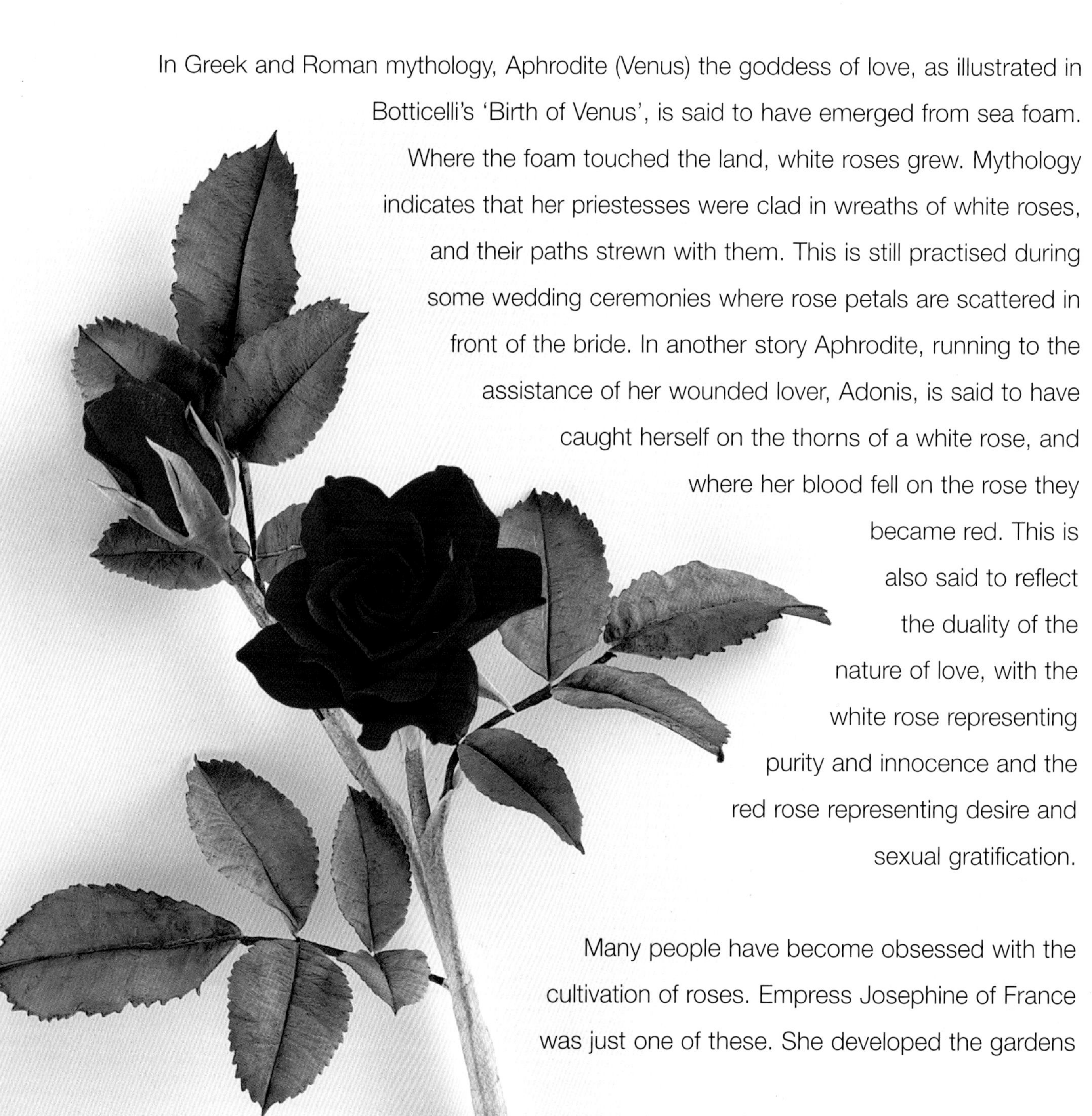

Many people have become obsessed with the cultivation of roses. Empress Josephine of France was just one of these. She developed the gardens

at Malmaison in, what is described by contemporary writers as, 'the English style'. Napoleon Bonaparte ordered his armies to collect roses from all areas, and even during hostilities the roses were given safe passage. The British Admiralty went so far as to issue orders that if a ship was carrying a cargo of roses or seeds for Malmaison, it was to be given immediate safe passage to its destination. Josephine engaged the services of many gardeners, horticulturists, botanists and artists. One of these was Pierre Joseph Redouté, a Belgian artist working in France. He immortalized Malmaison in his 'Jardin de Malmaison'. Today his name is forever remembered for his detailed paintings of old French roses, which have been reproduced many times.

The beauty of roses is not their only virtue. They also have many culinary uses and have been used through the centuries for making many simples and medicines. The growing and hybridization of roses is still very important. Each year new roses are launched at the major gardening events in North America, Britain and Europe. There is fierce competition between the many producers. There are few gardens that do not contain at least one, if not more roses.

Despite the popularity of the rose amongst cake decorators and sugarcrafters, this flower still remains one of the most difficult flowers to make consistently lifelike in sugar and cold porcelain. We hope that this book will help many sugarcrafters, both experienced and novice, to improve the making of their roses.

Warren, Peck 'n' Dunn

TRADITIONAL ROSES

Dog roses have always been one of my favourite flowers and I often use them on cakes for special occasions. With their understated elegance and wild charm, they make ideal flowers for decorating engagement cakes or trailing across a country-themed wedding cake. – *Tony*

Wild at Heart

Cake and Decoration

20cm (8in) heart-shaped cake
Apricot glaze
850g (1¾lb) white almond paste (marzipan)
Clear alcohol (kirsch or Cointreau)
1.26kg (2¾lb) ivory sugarpaste (cold rolled fondant)
30cm (12in) heart-shaped cake board
Pink ribbon to trim cake and cake board
Ivory royal icing
Piping gel

Flowers

7 full Dog roses
3 half Dog roses
9 Dog rosebuds
5 stems of 7 leaves
3 stems of 5 leaves

Equipment

Nos. 0 and 1 piping tubes (tips)
Dog rose embroidery template (see page 151)
Small flat dusting brush
Lace template (see page 151)
A4 plastic file pocket

PREPARATION

1 Brush the cake with apricot glaze and cover with almond paste. Leave to dry overnight. Moisten the almond paste with clear alcohol and cover with sugarpaste, using sugarpaste smoothers to achieve a good finish. Cover the board with sugarpaste and position the cake on top. Ensure a neat join between cake base and board.

2 Attach a thin band of ribbon to the base of the cake with a tiny amount of royal icing. Fit a piping bag with a no.1 tube and pipe a snail trail design of royal icing around the base of the cake. Secure a band of ribbon to the edge of the board using double-sided tape.

SIDE DESIGN

3 Trace the Dog rose embroidery side design template from page 151 onto greaseproof (parchment) paper. Scribe the design onto the side of the cake. Mix a little piping gel into the royal icing and insert it into a piping bag fitted with a no. 1 tube. Starting with the petals furthest away, pipe a line around the shape of the petal. Then take a small flat dusting brush moistened with water and gently brush the icing from the petal edge to the centre. Repeat for the rest of the petals, completing the design with the central petal.

4 Trace the lace design from page 151 onto tracing paper. Insert the paper with a piece of card into an A4 plastic file pocket. Pipe over the design with royal icing and no. 0 tube. Leave to dry. Scribe a fine line onto the cake to help position the lace. Attach the lace with two small dots of royal icing piped using a no. 1 tube.

ASSEMBLY

5 Form the spray as instructed on page 14. Taking care not to damage the lace, insert the handle of the spray into the pick before inserting it into the cake (this will ensure the pick does not disappear into the cake and be swallowed!). It may be easier to attach the lace after positioning the flowers.

Dog Rose

This is only one of the many wild roses native to Great Britain. They are a familiar sight to anyone who lives in the countryside, where they make a wonderful tapestry of colour in the hedgerows and are often found alongside honeysuckle, their mingled perfume being another wonderful attraction.

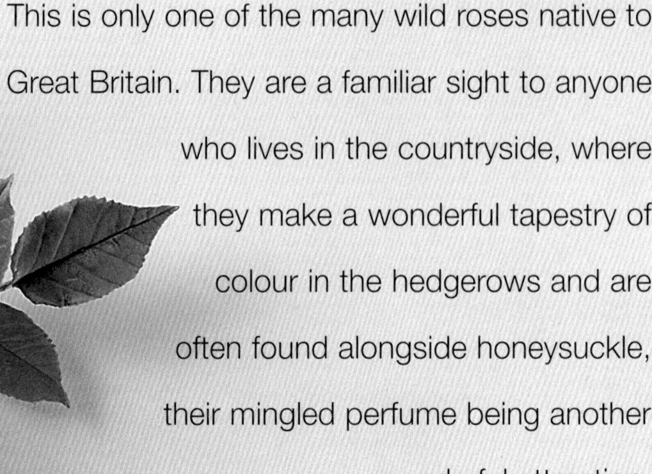

Materials

Fine 120-gauge white lace makers' thread (B120, APOC)

33-, 28-, 24- and 22-gauge white wires

Pale melon, pale green and mid-green flowerpaste (gum paste)

Primrose, white, lemon, vine green, pale pink, moss green and red petal dusts

White bridal satin dust

Half glaze

Equipment

Scriber tool (PME)

Silicone Plastique mould (see page 34)

Heart cutter (TT332)

Christmas rose veiner (GI)

Rose calyx cutter (OP R11)

Rose petal cutter (TT280)

Rose leaf cutter set (JL10)

Large briar rose leaf veiner (GI)

Nile green floristry tape

STAMENS

1 Wrap the fine white thread around two fingers about forty times. Remove the thread and twist the loop into a figure of eight, then fold over to make a smaller loop.

2 Insert a 33-gauge wire through the centre of the loop and fold over to hold the thread in place. Tape around the base of the thread adding a 22-gauge wire. Continue taping down to the end.

3 Cut open the loop and trim until it is slightly curved and shorter around the edges. Dip the thread into some fresh egg white then blot lightly. While the threads are still quite damp, separate them with the scriber tool and then bend them over slightly towards the centre. Allow to dry.

4 Separate the stamens with the scriber tool and dust them with a mixture of primrose and white petal dusts. Moisten the stamen tips with egg white and dip into lemon petal dust to form the pollen.

CENTRE AND PETALS

5 You will first need to make a mould from the centre of a real Dog rose using the Silicone Plastique or other chosen modelling material as described on page 34. Roll a small ball of pale melon flowerpaste and place into the mould, removing it carefully with the scriber. Moisten the base and stick into the centre of the stamens. Dust lightly with vine green petal dust.

6 Roll out the pale melon flowerpaste leaving a small ridge at one end. Cut out five petals with the heart-shaped cutter with the point of the heart over the ridge. Moisten the end of a 28-gauge wire and insert into the ridge. Soften the edges with a large celstick. Place the petals in the Christmas rose veiner, press firmly, remove and then, using a cocktail stick (toothpick), roll back the top edges of the petals to create a natural shape. Place on dimpled foam to dry. Dust the base of each petal lightly with primrose and the top edges with pale pink petal dust. Tape the five petals around the stamens, making sure the

moistened 24-gauge wire. Leave to dry. Roll out some pale melon flowerpaste and cut out four petals using the small rose petal cutter. Place the petals on a celpad and soften the edges using the rounded edge of the large celstick.

11 Moisten the whole of one petal and place it around the dried cone, slightly higher than the cone itself. Wrap the left-hand side of the petal in towards the cone, hiding the tip completely, then wrap the other side around it to form a tight spiral, but leaving the end open slightly. Moisten the bases of the last three petals. Attach and tuck the first of these into the open edge of the first

last petal is underneath the others on either side of it.

CALYX

7 Shape a piece of pale green flowerpaste into a cone and pinch out the base to form a hat shape. Using a small celstick, roll out the base to make it thinner. Cut out the calyx and elongate each sepal.

8 With curved scissors, make fine cuts down the edges of the sepals to create the calyx hairs. As this is a species rose, the hairs on the edges of the calyces are of a specific number. The old country saying bears this out: 'Two with two, two without, one with one and one without'. This means that on two of the sepals you cut two fine hairs on each side, the two alternate sepals have no hairs and the fifth one has one hair on one side and none on the other. Place on a celpad and cup the inside part using the rounded end of a celstick. Dust the inside of the calyx with white bridal satin.

9 Moisten the centre of the calyx and attach to the back of the rose, positioning the sepals between the petals. Curl the tips of the sepals back slightly. Dust the back of the sepals with moss green and the edges with red.

BUDS

10 Make a small cone with pale melon flowerpaste and insert a hooked,

petal on the cone. Then place the second and third evenly around to form a tight spiral. For the rosebud calyx, follow the same instructions as for the full rose calyx and wrap it tightly around the bud. Do not curl back the sepal tips.

LEAVES

12 As this is a species rose, the leaflets are usually made up of seven leaves or occasionally five leaves, the larger being at the tip. Roll out some mid-green flowerpaste, leaving a thick ridge down the centre. Cut out one large leaf, two sets of leaves with the middle-sized cutter, and two leaves with the smaller cutter for a seven-leaf stem. Miss out the two smaller leaves if you are making a five-leaf stem. Make sure the ridge is down the centre length of the leaves. Insert a moistened 28-gauge wire into the ridge of each leaf, making sure it goes in at least halfway up the length of the leaf. Place onto a celpad and soften the edges with the rounded end of a celstick. Press the leaf into the briar rose leaf veiner, then carefully pinch a vein down the centre. Repeat for the other leaves. Twist the leaves slightly with your fingers to give a variety of shapes.

13 Use a flat brush to dust the centre of the leaves with lemon petal dust, then overdust with moss green. The backs of the leaves should be paler than the upper surface. Overdust them with a little green dust lightened with white if they have become too dark. Dip the leaves into half glaze. Leave to dry. Tape the leaves together, using half-width nile green floristry tape, in groups of five or seven, starting with a large leaf and finishing with the smaller ones.

ASSEMBLING THE SPRAY

14 Tape the roses and rosebuds into groups of two to five to each stem. Keep a few single roses to fill in any spaces later. Tape the rose groups to the leaf stems, arranging them so that the full roses are in the centre. Leave a longer stem on the end to trail down the side of the cake. Cut away excess wires and tape over to make a neat handle.

This unusual Christmas cake is inspired by the Medieval practice of gathering rose hips for medicinal purposes, and the habit of feeding livestock on ivy during the bleak winter months when no other fodder was available. I have used the appleberries to complement and complete this design. *–Alan*

Medieval Harvest Medley

Cake and Decoration

15cm (6in) round cake and 23cm (9in) board
Apricot glaze
500g (1lb) white almond paste (marzipan)
Clear alcohol (kirsch or Cointreau)
500g (1lb) champagne sugarpaste (cold rolled fondant)
Broad orange satin ribbon to trim cake
Royal icing (optional)
Ribbed orange ribbon to trim board
Small amount of flowerpaste (gum paste)
Red, tangerine and holly/ivy petal dusts

Flowers

10 *Rosa rugosa* hips
7 sets of *Rosa rugosa* leaves
5 stems of purple appleberries
3 trailing ivy stems (see page 77)

Equipment

Thorn cutter (J)
Ornate candle holder
Nile green floristry tape
Posy pick

PREPARATION

1 Brush the cake with apricot glaze and cover with almond paste. Allow to dry for one week. Moisten the surface of the almond paste with clear alcohol and cover with champagne sugarpaste, using sugarpaste smoothers in order to create a good, smooth finish. Cover the cake board with sugarpaste and then position the cake on top. Use the smoothers again to press firmly on the cake to secure it to the board. Allow to dry for a few days.

2 Attach a broad band of orange satin ribbon around the base of the cake, using either royal icing or some sugarpaste softened with clear alcohol to about the same consistency as royal icing. Attach a band of ribbed orange ribbon to the board edge, using a non-toxic glue stick.

THORN SIDE DESIGN

3 Roll out some well-kneaded flower-paste and cut out a series of thorns using the cutter (there are various sizes on the cutter). Carefully remove the thorns from the cutter, pinch their tips into a sharper point, then attach to the cake, using either a tiny amount of royal icing or softened sugarpaste.

4 Allow to dry and then dust the thorns very carefully with a mixture of red and tangerine petal dusts. Add a little holly/ivy petal dust every now and then, too!

ASSEMBLY

5 The candle holder pictured has four cattle heads, making it perfect to rest the cake at an angle. Position the cake tilted at an angle of approximately 45°, as pictured.

6 Tape together a wild spray of rose hips and purple appleberries. Insert the handle of the spray into a posy pick, and then into the cake. Arrange some ivy and fruit at the base of the cake to balance the display.

Rosa Rugosa Hips

Rosa rugosa produces plump, orangey rose hips that vary slightly in size and shape, some round and others quite flattened. The leaves have wonderfully coarse-textured veining.

Materials

Fine 120-gauge lace makers' thread (B120, APOC)

24-gauge wire

Nutkin brown, black, red, tangerine, holly/ivy, vine green, forest green and aubergine petal dusts

Holly/ivy and cream flowerpaste (gum paste)

Half and full glaze

Equipment

Emery board

Rose calyx cutter (OP R12)

Black rose leaf set cutters (J)

***Rosa rugosa* leaf veiners (GI)**

Nile green floristry tape

STAMENS AND CALYX

1 Wrap fine lace makers' thread around two slightly parted fingers several times, according to the planned size of hip. Remove from your fingers and twist the loop of thread into a figure of eight shape, then in half again to form a smaller loop. Bend a length of 24-gauge wire through the centre of the loop and tape the base of the loop tightly against the wire. Repeat this process at the opposite side of the loop to make two sets of stamens. Cut the thread through the centre and shorten both sets.

2 Fuzz up the tips of the thread with an emery board. Dust the stamens with nutkin brown and black petal dusts. Singe the tips of the thread slightly, using a naked flame.

3 To make the calyx, pinch a cone of holly/ivy flowerpaste into a hat shape and thin out the base with a celstick. Cut out the calyx using the rose calyx cutter. Pinch each sepal between finger and thumb for sharper points, then elongate and thin out the sepals again.

4 Open up the calyx centre using the pointed end of a celstick. Cup the base of each sepal with a small metal ball tool. Pinch a central vein down each sepal, keeping the tips very sharp. Using some fine scissors, snip fine hairs from the sepal edges. Moisten the calyx centre and thread the stamens through the centre. Pinch the sepals up around the stamens. Allow to dry.

HIPS AND LEAVES

5 Roll a ball of cream and holly/ivy flowerpaste. Open the centre using the pointed end of a celstick. Moisten the base of the calyx with egg white and thread the wire through the centre of the ball of paste. Pinch off any excess.

6 Before the paste dries out, dust the main body of the hip with red and tangerine petal dusts. (Add holly/ivy and vine green dusts for unripe fruit.) Dust the outside of the calyx with vine green and holly/ivy. Allow to dry, then glaze with a full glaze. Bend the stem towards and past the calyx to dip. Glaze the fruit, up to the join with the calyx.

7 Cut out the leaves in sets of five or seven and vein each leaf. Dust the front of each leaf heavily with forest green and holly/ivy petal dust. Add a small amount of aubergine dust to the edges. Glaze using a half glaze. Tape the leaves into sets of five or seven.

Purple Appleberries (*Billardiera longiflora*)

This curious climbing plant originates from South-Eastern Australia. The flowers are a pale yellowish-green with a purple tinge to the petal edges. The fruit ripens to a wonderful intense purple, making it an attractive addition to autumn arrangements.

Materials

33-, 26- and 22-gauge white wires

Deep purple and holly/ivy flowerpaste (gum paste)

African violet, deep purple, aubergine, forest green and foliage petal dusts

Half and full glaze

Equipment

Sharp scalpel or plain-edged cutting wheel (PME)

Nile green floristry tape

BERRIES

1 To form the berry shape, cut short lengths of 33-gauge wire and hook them at one end. Roll out a small ball of purple flowerpaste and insert a hooked wire moistened with egg white. Re-model the shape until it resembles a slightly pointed and elongated apple.

2 Divide each berry into three fairly even sections, running from the tip down to the base of the berry. Use either a sharp scalpel or a plain-edged cutting wheel in order to form the dividing lines. Texture the surface of the berry in between each of the main divisions.

COLOURING THE BERRIES

3 Before the berries have had a chance to dry out, dust them with African violet and deep purple petal dusts. Catch the tip and the base of the fruit with a small amount of aubergine dust. Leave the berries to dry and then dip them into a full glaze. Tape over each stem with quarter-width nile green floristry tape.

LEAVES

4 The leaves are made using a quick method, which I like to call the 'splat' method! Roll a small sausage of holly/ivy paste onto a 33-gauge white wire. Then work the paste up into a point at the end of the wire.

5 Flatten the leaf shape using the flat side of any of your leaf or petal veiners. If the leaf is a little on the thick side, then soften the edges slightly against a pad using either a metal ball tool or the rounded end of a celstick. Pinch the leaf firmly from the base to the tip to accentuate a central vein. Dust with forest green and foliage petal dusts. Dip into a half glaze.

6 Tape the leaves onto 26-gauge wire using quarter-width nile green floristry tape. Gradually introduce the berries, adding a single leaf with each one. To form a long stem, tape smaller stems onto a 22-gauge wire. Bend the tips of each group to provide more movement to the arrangement.

This two-tier summer wedding cake illustrates just how effective a few well chosen roses combined with a large quantity of foliage can be. The cake has been simply decorated with a broad band of decorative leaf design ribbon and a scattering of tiny yellow petals. –*Alan*

Golden Days

Cake and Decoration

20cm (8in) and 25cm (10in) elliptical cakes

Apricot glaze

20cm (8in) and 36cm (14in) elliptical cake boards (these will need to be ordered)

2kg (4½lb) white almond paste (marzipan)

Clear alcohol (kirsch or Cointreau)

3kg (6½lb) sugarpaste (cold rolled fondant)

Bitter lemon paste food colouring

Small amount of pale yellow flowerpaste (gum paste)

Broad, leaf design ribbon to trim cake

Royal icing (optional)

Green ribbon to trim board

Flowers

3 full 'Golden Wings' roses

4 'Golden Wings' rosebuds

20 sets of rose leaves

Equipment

Two long tapered crystal pillars

Nile green floristry tape

2 posy picks

PREPARATION

1 First of all, position the smaller cake onto the self-sized board, and then brush both cakes with apricot glaze. Next, cover each of the cakes with a layer of almond paste, making sure that the edge of the board is completely covered with almond paste. Allow to dry for a few days.

2 Moisten the surface of each cake with clear alcohol and cover with sugarpaste, having first coloured the sugarpaste with bitter lemon paste food colouring. Cover the large base board with the same coloured sugarpaste and then position the larger cake on top. Leave to dry for a few days.

3 Attach a broad band of decorative ribbon to the sides of both cakes, using a very small amount of royal icing or sugarpaste softened with clear alcohol.

4 Insert two long tapered crystal pillars into the base tier. Then position the smaller cake at an angle on top of the crystal pillars as shown. If you are worried about using a real cake, then one alternative is to use a polystyrene dummy cake for the top tier and then provide extra cutting cake to serve at the wedding reception. Glue a band of green ribbon to the edge of the base board using a non-toxic glue stick.

ASSEMBLY

5 To form the cascading spray, tape together three separate rose stems. Insert the top and middle sprays into posy picks inserted into each cake. Position the third spray at the base of the larger cake.

6 As a final decorative touch, roll out a little pale yellow flowerpaste and cut out some tiny, rose petal shapes. Now soften the edges of these petals, cup and then attach to the cakes, in a few light scatterings across both tiers, with a tiny dot of either royal icing or softened sugarpaste.

'Golden Wings'

'Golden Wings' is a single-flowered shrub rose with large, pale yellow blooms that generally consist of only five petals. I am not usually a big fan of yellow flowers, but this plant holds a particular attraction for me, partly due to its curious, red-tinged stamens that create an interesting focal point to the flower. 'Golden Wings' is a hybrid rose that was created in the USA in 1956 and is a relative of the very hardy Scottish burnet rose, which helps to explain its long flowering and tough resistance to both wind and rainy conditions!

Equipment

Large rose petal cutters (TT276, 277)
Very large rose petal veiner (GI)
Large ball tool (optional)
Ceramic silk veining tool (HP)
Rose calyx cutters (OP R11, 11a)
Pointed rose leaf cutters (J)
Large tea rose leaf veiner (GI)
Nile green floristry tape
Non-toxic hi-tack glue

Materials

28- or 26-, 22- and 20-gauge white wires
Mid-holly/ivy and pale lemon flowerpaste
Small seedhead stamens
Vine green, lemon, red, primrose, white, holly/ivy, forest green and aubergine petal dusts
Half glaze

STAMENS

1 Using a pair of fine-nosed pliers, bend an open loop in the end of a 22-gauge white wire. Bend the loop back against the wire and then, holding the loop and part of the length with the pair of pliers, bend it once again at right angles to form a shape like a ski stick, with the wire descending from the centre of the loop. Attach a small ball of mid-holly/ivy flowerpaste onto the centre of the loop and texture the ball with the point of a scalpel blade. Allow to dry completely.

2 You will need to use between a third of a bunch and half a bunch of seedhead stamens for each flower. Take several small groups of stamens, line up their heads and then glue the stamens at the centre using some hi-tack non-toxic glue. Squeeze and spread the glue into the length of the group, leaving part of the length and tips unglued at either end.

3 Allow to firm a little before cutting the group in half and trimming off the excess from the base of each new group. Repeat this process until you have several groups – enough to form a good ring of stamens around the centre.

4 Next, apply some more glue to the base of each small group and carefully attach to the ski-stick wire. Try not to get too much glue onto the sugar as this may dissolve it. As an alternative to using the non-toxic glue, you could use some softened flowerpaste.

5 Squeeze the stamens against the wire to get them to bond. You will now need to repeat the process until you have attached enough stamens to form a good ring. Allow to dry.

PETALS

7 Decide which size flower you want to make and then squeeze the cutter to make the shape a little narrower (see also petal templates on page 154).

9 Using the pointed end of the rose petal cutter, bite out a 'V'-shape from the top of the petal. Round off the 'V'-shape using a fine pair of scissors. Place the petal on a pad and soften the edges slightly.

10 Place the petal into the large rose petal veiner and press very firmly to give the maximum veining to the petal. Cup either side of the central vein with finger and thumb or with a large ball tool or the rounded end of a large celstick.

11 Soften the edges further, if required, using the ceramic silk veining tool. Allow the petal to firm up a little over a cupped former. Repeat this process to make five petals for each flower (although some variation has been known to occur, so add a sixth petal to one of your roses if you so desire).

COLOURING

12 Dust each of the petals from the base to the tip with a mixture of primrose and lemon blended together with a touch of white dust. Add a touch of vine green at the base of each petal.

6 Using a fine pair of tweezers, curl the stamens from the base out and then back in again. Dust the paste centre with a touch of vine green petal dust and then dust the tips of the stamens with some lemon petal dust. Dust the filaments with red petal dust.

8 Roll out some pale lemon flowerpaste, leaving a thick ridge. Cut out a petal shape with one of the two cutters. Insert a moistened 26-gauge wire into the ridge and pinch the base of the petal down onto the wire to secure and elongate the final shape.

ASSEMBLY

13 To assemble the flower, tape the petals around the stamens using some half-width nile green floristry tape. The petals should still be slightly damp so that you can re-shape them and curl their edges back if you need to.

CALYX

14 Roll a ball of holly/ivy paste into a cone shape and then pinch out the base to form a hat shape. Roll out the paste to make it a little finer, although the paste should still be slightly fleshy when you finish.

15 Cut out the calyx shape using the larger rose calyx cutter and then, using a celstick, elongate each of the sepals by rolling them against the board.

16 Place the calyx onto a pad and cup the centre of each sepal. Dust the inside of the calyx with a mixture of holly/ivy and white petal dusts to make it paler and give it a velvety texture. Using a pair of fine scissors, add some fine cuts to all bar one of the sepals. (There is no exact number as this is a hybrid flower and only true species roses have an exact number of hairs to each sepal.)

17 Open up the centre of the calyx using the pointed end of the celstick and then moisten the centre and thread the calyx onto the back of the rose. You should position each sepal so that it covers a gap in the petals. Curl the tips of the calyx back slightly in order to create a more natural finish.

18 Dust the tips of the calyx with red petal dust, then darken the remainder of each of the sepals using a combination of forest, holly/ivy and vine green petal dusts. Paint with half glaze when dry if required or if time allows.

BUDS

19 Bend a hook in the end of a 20-gauge wire. Form a basic rose cone shape, making sure it is not too large, then insert the moistened wire into the base. Roll out some lemon flowerpaste and cut out five small petals. Soften the edges slightly.

20 Moisten the first petal and wrap it around the cone, leaving some of the petal length above the bud. Wrap the petal into a tight spiral, leaving one end open ready to tuck the next petal underneath. Take the third petal, tuck it under the second petal and then spiral it again, leaving one petal open to tuck the fourth petal underneath. Add the last petal under the fourth in order to create the final spiral. Curl back the edges.

21 Add a calyx as for the flower but using the smaller rose calyx cutter. Dust the buds a stronger yellow than the flowers.

LEAVES

22 The leaves grow in sets of three, five or seven. Cut out the leaves using the basic leaf method and the pointed leaf cutters. Insert 28- or 26-gauge wires depending upon the size of each leaf.

23 Soften the edges and vein using the large tea rose veiner. You will need to position the leaves near to the tip of the veiner to obtain good veining for the size of leaves you are using.

24 Dust the edges and the central vein of each leaf with a mixture of aubergine and red petal dust. Overdust in layers with forest, holly/ivy and vine green petal dusts. Try to keep the backs of each leaf much paler than the front. Add a touch of white to the backs if necessary. Dip into a half glaze and then tape up the leaves into their sets. When you tape up a main rose stem, do remember to add leaves each time you add either a bud or a flower.

25 Dust the main stems of the leaves with a combination of the aubergine, red and green petal dusts. If you wish, you can seal the stems by rubbing them with a small amount of hi-tack non-toxic glue. The hi-tack glue will dry clear.

Glass arrangement: This is a display suggestion for a floral competition piece. The 'Golden Wings' roses have been carefully positioned at the rim and the base of the glass.

The item that started this project was the snowberries. I had wanted to incorporate snowberries into an arrangement for some time. The shimmering leaves of the white poplar had also fascinated me. The creamy-white Bourbon rose 'Boule de neige' just cried out to be included! *–Tombi*

White Christmas

Flowers

3 full 'Boule de neige' roses

2 'Boule de neige' rosebuds

5 stems of white poplar

5 stems of snowberries

2 stems of *Miltonia flavescens* plus 1 extra flower

2 *Miltonia flavescens* buds

Materials and Equipment

20- and 18-gauge wires

Nile green floristry tape

Suitable container

Florists' staysoft

PREPARATION

1 You will first of all need to strengthen any of the flowers or stems of poplar and snowberries that might need extra support. This can be done by taping in additional 20- or 18-gauge wires to the existing stems.

2 Place a piece of well-kneaded staysoft into the container, pressing it firmly down to make sure that it is secure and that the weight is evenly distributed to support the arrangement. I have used a small green glass bowl for a container, but any container you wish to use, provided it is large enough, will be suitable.

ASSEMBLY

3 The first stage is to insert the stems of white poplar into the staysoft to form the basic outline of the arrangement. These poplar stems will define the overall height and width of the design, so it is important to get their position exactly right.

4 Next add the stems of snowberries, which should follow the positions of the poplar stems. Leave one stem for the centre. Now add the stems of orchids. By adding several orchids to the arrangement, I have tried to offer a contrast to the rounded shapes of the roses and snowberries.

5 Finally, place the 'Boule de neige' roses in position and complete the arrangement with the rosebuds, the single orchid and the centrally placed stem of snowberries.

6 If you wanted to use this arrangement as the centrepiece for a dinner table, the elements would need to be arranged 'in the round' and the arrangement kept low. There aren't many occasions today when a tall arrangement is required for a dinner table. Very few meals are now so formal that you talk only to the people seated on either side of you, with tall arrangements and great silver epergnes being the order of the day!

'Boule de Neige'

An old garden rose that is considered by some rose lovers to be the most perfect white rose ever raised. The blooms are regular and symmetrical, and the the centre is softened by a hint of ivory.

Materials

28-, 26-, 24- and 18-gauge wires

White and pale green flowerpaste (gum paste)

Lemon yellow, vine, holly/ivy and forest green petal dusts

White bridal satin dust

Half glaze

Equipment

Rose petal cutters (TT276, 551, 550, 549)

Smooth porcelain tool (HP)

Round rose petal veiner (GI)

Calyx cutter (OP R11)

Black rose leaf cutters large and medium (J)

Large pale green rose leaf cutter (J)

Large briar rose leaf veiner (GI)

Dimpled foam

Nile green floristry tape

ROSE

1 This rose does not have a cone. The name of the flower indicates that the buds and flowers should look like snowballs. In order to do this, the rose centres have to be round. For the roses and the larger buds, the ball should be 2.5cm (1in) in diameter. Smaller buds will require smaller balls.

2 Cut 18-gauge wires in half and hook the ends. Moisten the end of one of the wires, insert it into some of the white paste and fasten firmly to the wire, keeping the ball shape. Allow to dry. It is imperative that these centres are thoroughly dry before you attempt to make either the rose or the buds.

3 Using the smallest of the rose petal cutters, cut out five petals for each bud or flower centre. Ensure that you do not cut out too many shapes as you will need to work on them before the paste dries out.

4 Soften the edge of each petal on a foam pad using the metal ball tool. Moisten the ball and attach the petals around it, spiralling them. The last petal should tuck under the first. Using the smooth porcelain tool, roll back the edge of each petal slightly.

5 Add another layer of five petals that have been cut out with the same sized cutter. Soften the edge of the petals on the foam pad using a ball tool. This should be done very lightly as there cannot be any softening of the edges. This process will provide a formal shape to the centre of the rose, creating a deep indentation.

6 Vein with the rose petal veiner. Attach the petals to the ball using a little egg white, positioning the petals over the joins of the previous layer. Once again, ensure that the petals spiral around the ball. These petals should be markedly higher than the ones located on the tightly closed centre.

7 Add another layer of petals of the same size as the previous ones, preparing them in exactly the same way.

8 Using the next-sized cutter, work the petals in the same way as above, this time loosening the petals very slightly. This set of petals should be a little taller than the previous layer.

9 The next layer is the first one that is wired. These petals also differ from their predecessors in that they need to be heart-shaped and very cupped.

10 Roll out the white paste in a long sausage, then roll away from it, leaving a thickened piece of paste at one long edge. Cut out five petals for each layer. Using the 'V' end of the cutter, cut out a V from the centre of the petal, softening the resulting sharp corners. Place the petals on the foam pad and soften with a metal ball tool.

11 Cut a 26-gauge wire into quarters and hook one of the lengths. Moisten it and insert into the thickened paste. Dust the petal veiner, vein then soften the edge lightly using a frilling tool. Press your thumb firmly into the centre of the petal to cup it well. This will lose some of the veining but it is important to keep the petals cupped.

12 For a fuller rose, add one or two more layers of heart-shaped petals. Each layer of petals should be slightly taller than the previous ones and still remain cupped. Place in an apple tray in order to set.

13 Repeat step 10 and cut out five petals using the larger sized rose petal cutter. Insert a moistened, hooked 26-gauge wire into the thickened paste. Place on the foam pad and soften the edges. Vein the petals, then place them in an apple tray in order to set.

14 Repeat the above process to create another identical layer of petals, but this time rolling back the edges of the petals in an attractive way. For a fuller rose, add an extra layer. The real roses have around 50 petals.

15 Dust a very small amount of lemon yellow at the base of each of the wired petals. Add a touch of vine green dust to the wire.

16 Tape the petals onto the centre of the rose using half-width nile green floristry tape. Ensure that you always tape the next layer over the join of the previous one. Arrange the petals in an attractive way.

CALYX

17 Roll a piece of pale green paste to form a cone, pinching out the broad end into a circle. Place the cone on your board. Roll out the paste using a celstick. Ensure that the pedicel is narrow enough to fit through the centre

of the calyx cutter. Cut out the shape and elongate each sepal. Using scissors, cut the edges of the sepals to make fine hairs.

18 Place the calyx on the foam pad and, on the inside of each sepal, mark a vein down its centre with the veiner. Repeat the veining process, this time using a dresden tool. Use the back of a celstick to make an indentation into the centre of the calyx.

19 Dust the inside of the calyx with white bridal satin. Moisten with egg white and attach the calyx to the back of the rose.

20 Run a small celstick around the base of the calyx to make a light indentation. This will form the hip of the calyx.

21 Dust the back of the calyx with some holly/ivy dust, ensuring that you leave a pale rim around each sepal. Steam the entire rose to set the dust. Set aside to dry.

BUD

22 To make a rosebud, add another few petals to a centre of white paste. This second layer should be more loosened than the first. Add a calyx to the bud as described above.

LEAVES

23 Roll out a piece of pale green paste over a groove in a board, choosing the appropriate size of groove for the thickness of wire used. Cut a 28-gauge wire into quarters to use for the small leaves. Moisten the wire and lay along the light line of the groove. Roll in and fold back in order to sandwich the wire between the layers of paste.

24 Cut out the leaf shapes and place them on the foam pad in order to soften the edges. Vein the leaves with the large briar rose leaf veiner and set them on some dimpled foam to dry. To form each group of leaves, you will need one large, two medium and two small leaves. Tape short lengths of the 24-gauge wires below each individual leaf to form the stalks.

25 Before the leaves are thoroughly dry, dust them with layers of holly/ivy and forest green dusts. Ensure that the underside of the leaf is paler than the top surface. Once the leaves are dry, glaze them with half glaze, then allow them to dry once more.

ASSEMBLY

26 Tape the leaves into groups using the nile green floristry tape. Arrange these newly formed groups around both the buds and the roses.

White Poplar

When I cut twigs from a white poplar tree I was absolutely amazed that there was no silvery finish to the leaves. They have a stark, matt, velvety finish to the underside of the leaves; the upper surface of the dark green leaves is also completely matt.

Materials

Silicone Plastique or modelling compound of your choice

White and green flowerpaste (gum paste)

30-, 28- and 22-gauge wires

Cornflour (cornstarch)

Holly/ivy, forest green and black petal dusts

Quarter glaze

Equipment

Home made leaf veiners (see page 34)

White floristry tape

1 You will first need to produce your own veiners as no veiners for these leaves have been made commercially. Follow steps on page 34 to make your own.

2 There is a tiny leaflet at the start of each stem. It is best to cut this by hand. Roll a small ball of paste into a cone, insert a 30-gauge wire into the point of the cone and flatten the paste. Use a sharp pair of scissors to cut a small tri-lobed leaf. Repeat this twice more, making smaller leaves.

3 Roll out white flowerpaste over a groove in a board, using the correct size of groove for the thickness of the wire. Moisten a 28-gauge wire, if you are making a small leaf, and place it along the pale line of the groove. Roll it in with a rolling pin, then bend back the flap of paste, sandwiching the wire between the two layers of paste. For larger leaves, increase the gauge of the wire.

4 Dust the veiner with cornflour, place the line formed by the groove along the central vein and then press the veiners together. Remove the paste from the veiner and cut away the excess paste, either with a pair of scissors or with a sharp craft knife. I find that a flicking motion with the knife cuts away the paste very satisfactorily.

5 Place the leaf on dimpled foam to set. When the leaf is holding its shape but is not yet dry, dust the leaf with holly/ivy green and forest green petal dusts, being extremely careful not to get any colour on the underside of the leaf. Glaze the leaf with a quarter glaze.

ASSEMBLY

6 Start off the stem by taping the three small leaflets together at the end of a 22-gauge wire. Tape using some white floristry tape.

7 The leaves are closer together towards the tip, and as the leaves get larger so do the gaps between the leaves. The leaves should also be alternate and spiralled around the stem. Rub the floristry tape with the back of a pair of scissors to give the tape a sheen.

Miltonia Flavescens

Unlike many others in its genus, this particular flower is not one of the pansy-faced orchids. Its lovely, creamy-green colouring embellishes this display superbly. Tony was the first to make this lovely orchid, and I am grateful that he generously allowed me to use my version in this arrangement.

Materials

White and very pale green flowerpaste (gum paste)

28-, 26-, 24- and 20-gauge white wires

Lemon, holly/ivy and vine green petal dusts

Poinsettia liquid colour (SK)

Equipment

Long leaf, simple leaf and cattleya sepal cutters (TT666, 225, 8)

Curved tweezers

Medium amaryllis veiner (GI)

Dimpled foam

Nile green floristry tape

COLUMN

1 Make a small cone out of some of the white paste. Moisten half the length of a 24-gauge white wire with a little egg white and insert it into the pointed end of the cone. Re-shape the cone and then hollow one of its sides, using a dresden tool to do this, so that you can also frill the sides of the column. Push the small end of a metal ball tool into the front of the column so that you end up with a hollow. Next, roll a tiny ball of white paste and attach it just inside the newly formed hollow at the front of the column. Mark this in half with a sharp craft knife. Then curve the column. Set the column aside to dry while you work on the rest of the flower.

LIP

2 Roll out a quantity of the white flowerpaste on a suitable sized groove. Moisten a 26-gauge white wire with egg white and place it along the pale groove. Roll the wire into the paste. Fold back the flap of paste, sandwiching the wire between the two layers. Roll out the paste again. Cut out the lip using the simple leaf cutter (TT225), positioning the broader end of the cutter over the paste at the edge of the board. Remove excess paste, place the cut out shape onto the centre of the amaryllis veiner, positioning it so that the veins ray out towards the tip of the lip. Remove from the veiner and work the edge of the lip with a dresden tool, then place on a foam pad and flute with a metal ball tool. Using the curved tweezers pinch two strong lines to form the callus, which is positioned just below the column. Twist gently to get some movement into the lip. Place on dimpled foam to set.

DORSAL PETALS

3 Roll out pale green paste over the groove, moisten and position a one-third length 28-gauge white wire along the groove, ensuring that it is about two-thirds the length of the petal. Sandwich the petal and wire together. Cut out the petal using the long leaf cutter (TT666) but only use two-thirds of the length of the cutter. Trim the base of the petals neatly. Place on the dimpled foam to set, gently soften the edge of the petals and use the veiner end of the dresden tool to mark a groove down the centre of each petal. Set on dimpled foam. The petals should curve back gently.

SEPALS

4 Roll out pale green flowerpaste over the groove and cut out with the long leaf

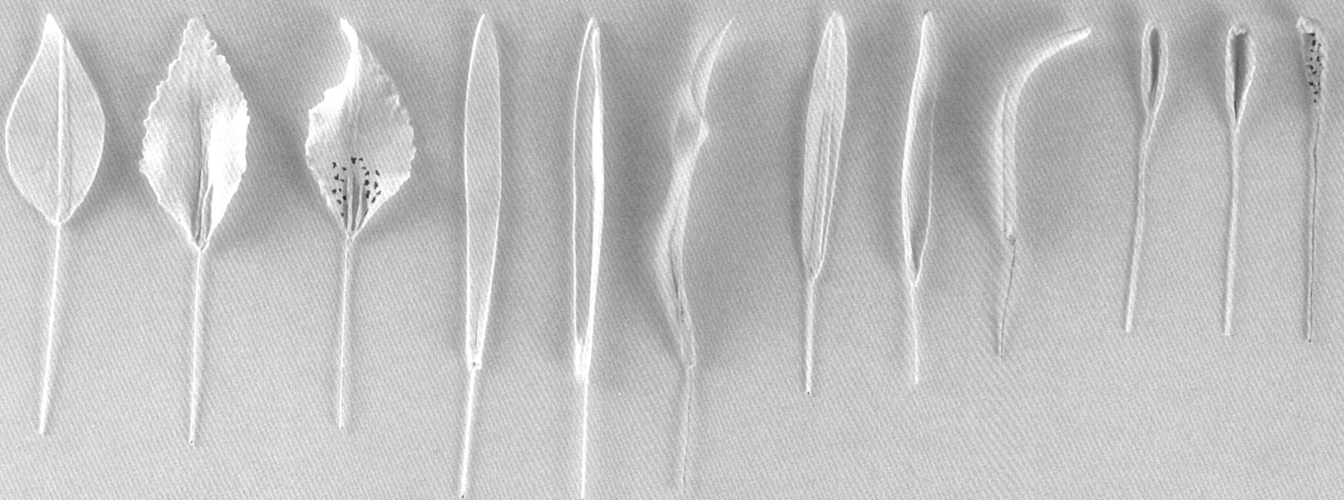

cutter. Insert a moistened one-third length 26-gauge white wire, which should extend to approximately two-thirds of the length of the sepal. Cut out three sepals this way, place them on the foam pad, soften the edges and create a groove down the centre of each. Set the sepals on the dimpled foam to set. The dorsal sepals should be curved so they have 'bandy legs' and the lateral sepal should curve back gently.

5 Roll out pale green paste over the fine groove on the board, moisten a quarter length 28-gauge wire and place it along the pale groove. Turn back the paste and roll it out again, sandwiching the wire between the two layers of paste.

6 Cut out a dorsal petal with cutter TT666, using only two thirds of the cutter length. Trim the squared-off base into a gentle point with sharp scissors. Soften the edge of the petals on a foam pad using a metal ball tool. Run a veiner down the centre of the petal to make a central vein. Place onto dimpled foam to dry, curving the petal back gently. Repeat this for the second petal.

BUDS

7 Roll a small cone of pale green paste. Insert a hooked, moistened 26-gauge white wire into the broad end of the paste, work with your fingers to elongate the point, insert into a 3 cage or mark three grooves onto the bud and then curve the tip gently. Leave to dry.

BRACTS

8 Each flower and bud has a bract. The bracts for the buds are cut using the TT8 cutter, with a 28-gauge moistened white wire in place. Soften the edges on the foam pad and mark a groove down the centre with the veiner. The smaller the bud, the smaller the bract needs to be. To make the bracts for the flowers after cutting out the shape, elongate the bract and vein it with the veining tool. Set to dry on dimpled foam.

COLOURING

9 When the column is dry, very carefully paint little spots on the underside using poinsettia liquid colour. Then when the lip is dry, dust the centre of the upper third of the lip with lemon petal dust. Paint small red spots around the callus and behind it as well. Some of these orchids also have lines raying from the centre. Dust the dorsal petals and sepals with vine green petal dust and lightly overdust with holly/ivy.

10 Now dust the bracts using exactly the same method, only this time ensure that they are a slightly deeper green than the petals. Highlight the buds with a dusting of vine green petal dust. Finally, dust a little of the holly/ivy petal dust into the grooves.

ASSEMBLY

11 Using nile green floristry tape, fix the lip below the column, then tape the dorsal petals on either side and behind the column. Tape the lateral sepal behind the dorsal petals and the lateral sepals to either side. Cut off excess wire and tape down the stem. Tape the bract about 1.25–2.5cm (½–1in) below the flower. Now steam the flower to set the dust. Then tape the bracts a little below the buds and steam again.

12 To assemble the stems, begin by taping the buds and bracts to the 20-gauge wire using nile green floristry tape. Make sure you increase the spaces between the buds as you go down the wire. Tape a good length down the wire before adding the first flower. Repeat the same process for all the other stems.

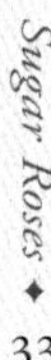

SNOWBERRIES

(*Symphoricarpos racemosus*)

A deciduous shrub that originates from North America – it bears slender, arching branches ending in pretty little bell-shaped flowers leading to rather translucent globular fruit.

Materials

Silicone Plastique or modelling compound of your choice

Cold cream

Cornflour (cornstarch)

Pale green and white flowerpaste (gum paste)

30-, 28-, 26-, 24- and 22-gauge wires

White bridal satin dust

Vine green, holly/ivy and forest green petal dusts

Quarter glaze

Dark brown or black liquid colour

Equipment

Home made leaf veiners

Piece of smooth, thick plastic

Plain-edged cutting wheel (PME)

Nile green, twig and white floristry tapes

MAKING YOUR OWN VEINERS

1 The first task is to make your veiners as no commercial veiners are available. If you are not familiar with the plant it is best to wait until the very noticeable berries appear in autumn.

2 Follow the instructions that come with the modelling compound of your choice. If using the Silicone Plastique, mix the compound and the curing agent together in equal proportions and work until no longer streaky. Mix enough for only one or two leaves at a time. (If you have to pause while working on the silicone, put the mixed compound in a plastic bag and place in the freezer to slow down the curing time.) Roll it into an oval and press it against the sheet of plastic to give a smooth, shiny surface. There are very few surfaces that this compound does not stick to so be very careful where you put it down. It actually sticks extremely well to non-stick boards! I place the pieces on cling film fastened over an old cake board.

3 Press the underside of the leaf against the silicone, starting with the central vein. Carefully make sure you trap no air bubbles under the leaf. Very quickly trim off the excess silicone, leaving just a narrow margin around the edge of the leaf. Roll up again and repeat the process for as many different leaves as are required. Leave to set completely.

The length of time this takes depends on the temperature of the room you are working in. Remove the leaf from the mould and carefully work cold cream into the veins. Do not leave a thick deposit of cream in the veins as this will spoil the finished veiner.

4 Mix another batch of moulding compound, a little less than before, to form the underside of the leaf. The modelling compound needs to be thicker for the underside as the veins are deeper. (If you are taking a mould from a leaf with a very frilled edge, it will require a lot more modelling paste to give the required depth).

5 Roll into an oval, press against the plastic to make the surface smooth and then, starting from the central vein, press the modelling compound into the veiner you have already made, once again being careful not to trap any air bubbles. This would spoil your finished veiner. Cut away the excess silicone and allow to set. Before the compound has set completely, it is wise to use a scriber to mark into the veiner the name of the plant from which it is taken and your initials, being careful not to mark it too vigorously and possibly damage the impression of the veins.

6 It is important before you use the veiner to wipe it carefully with a little kitchen paper and dust carefully with cornflour. You can now use it in the same way as a commercial veiner.

LEAVES

7 To make a leaf, roll out a piece of pale green flower paste on a grooved board. Moisten 28-gauge wires with egg white, then place the wire along the groove, roll it in, fold back the paste, and roll out again. Lift the wired paste and place the grooved back down the central vein. Press the top veiner onto the paste and press down firmly. Remove the veined paste from the veiner and, using either the plain-edged cutting wheel or a sharp pair of scissors, cut away the excess paste. Set the leaf to dry. The leaves of the plant are arranged in pairs from the stem, so all leaves should be made as pairs. Increase the size of wire you use as the leaves get larger. Make several tiny sets of leaves, using the 'splat' method. Take a very small piece of paste and roll it into a tiny cone. Then insert a moistened 30-gauge wire into the point of the cone and flatten it under something smooth (this is where the splat comes in) and vein on your smallest veiner. These small leaves usually emerge between several berries near the base of the raceme.

BUDS

8 Use 30-gauge wire cut into six short pieces. Roll tiny ovals of pale green paste, insert the moistened wire through the oval so that the wire protrudes. Work the paste onto the wire.

BERRIES

9 Make a series of small balls, some from very pale green paste. Continue, making others from white paste, increasing in size gradually. Insert moistened quarter-length 28-gauge wires through the balls. Once the balls are dry, cut off most of the extending wire, leaving only tiny protrusions.

COLOURING AND ASSEMBLY

10 Dust the balls with white bridal satin. Using a moistened brush, touch the protrusions lightly with diluted dark brown or black liquid colour. Dust the leaves with vine green and holly/ivy. The smaller the leaves the lighter the colouring. The larger leaves should be over-dusted with a little forest green dust to blend the other colours together. Create light and shade by varying the dusting. Glaze the leaves with quarter glaze, since flowerpaste is very matt and foliage in particular can look very dull if all the pieces are dusted similarly. Using quarter-width nile green floristry tape, tape between 10 and 12 of the green buds together, forming a 'tail', and lightly dust with a touch of vine green and holly/ivy. Tuck a half-length 22-gauge wire among the excess wires, and changing to half-width twig tape, tape it in and trim away some of the excess wires. Now add a few of the pale green round balls and a few larger white ones, with white tape. When you have a cluster you like, tape in two tiny green leaves together, the fronts of the leaves facing one another.

11 A few smaller balls finish off the cluster. Continue taping down the wire, adding pairs of leaves as you go. They spiral around the stem. Steam the clusters of snowberries to set the dust.

The old-fashioned roses on this cake are extremely delicate but also complex. The soft colouring will add a timeless beauty to even the simplest of designs. The subtle pink hues will add a romantic tone to a wedding cake, providing a royal touch to any festive occasion. –*Tony*

Danish Romance

Cake and Decoration

23cm (9in) round cake board

750g (1½lb) white sugarpaste (cold rolled fondant)

15cm (6in) round cake

Apricot glaze

360g (12oz) white almond paste (marzipan)

Clear alcohol (kirsch or Cointreau)

Pale green petal dust

Rose ribbon to trim cake

Royal icing

Rose ribbon to trim board

Flowers

3 full 'Queen of Denmark' roses

3 'Queen of Denmark' rosebuds

8 sets of rose leaves

Equipment

Fresh rose leaves for embossing

PREPARATION

1 Start by covering the cake board with some of the white sugarpaste. To create the embossed rose leaf effect, press the rose leaves around the edge of the board into the sugarpaste, which should still be quite soft. Allow the sugarpaste to dry.

2 Brush the cake with some warmed apricot glaze and then cover with white almond paste, using sugarpaste smoothers to obtain a smooth, polished finish. Leave the cake to dry overnight if possible.

3 Moisten the almond paste with the clear alcohol and cover with the remaining white sugarpaste. Use a combination of the sugarpaste smoothers and a small amount of softened sugarpaste to achieve a smooth finish to the cake surface.

4 Place the cake in a central position on the board. Emboss the top edge of the cake with the rose leaves in the same manner as for the cake board edge. Allow to dry once more.

5 Use pale green petal dust to colour the various embossed rose leaves on both the cake and the board, taking care not to use too much dust or to spray the dust over the leaf edges.

6 Fasten a band of ribbon around the base of the cake, securing it with a small amount of royal icing. Use double-sided tape to attach the ribbon to the board.

ASSEMBLY

7 For the top arrangement, tape together one full 'Queen of Denmark' rose, two rosebuds and five stems of leaves. Attach the spray to the top of the cake with a little royal icing. The side arrangement consists of two full roses, one bud and three stems of leaves. Use some royal icing to attach this side arrangement to one side of the cake board.

'Queen of Denmark'

This old-fashioned Alba rose has greyish-green foliage and bears beautiful scented pink flowers going deeper at the heart. The rose is made up in four sections with over forty petals to an open bloom.

Materials

Pale claret, pale green, white and mid-green flowerpaste (gum paste)

28-, 26-, 24-, 20- and 18-gauge wires

Pink, plum, violet, moss green and white petal dusts

Half glaze

Equipment

Rose petal cutters (TT276–278, 550–551)

Large rose petal veiner (GI)

Rose calyx cutters (OP R11 and R11b)

Rose leaf cutter (J L10)

Large rose leaf veiner (GI)

Nile green floristry tape

CONE

1 Moisten a hooked 24-gauge wire with egg white and insert it into a small ball of pale claret flowerpaste that has been flattened slightly. Allow to dry.

PETALS

2 Roll out pale claret flowerpaste and cut out two petals of each size petal cutter. Place the petals on a pad, soften the edges, then vein using the rose petal veiner.

3 Moisten the base of each of the petals and place the small, flattened ball of wired flowerpaste onto one side of the petal, near the base. Wrap the petal around and secure at the base. Wrap the second petal around the first, then slightly flatten the whole petal. You will need four wired petals altogether.

4 Tape together the four sections of petals using nile green floristry tape. It is better to do this while they are still soft as they will fit snugly against each other. The petals should be curving inwards and down towards the centre.

5 Roll out some more paste and cut out another four petals using a slightly larger cutter than in the previous step.

Place on a pad, soften the edges, then vein. Moisten the base of the petals and wrap one petal around each of the sections, tucking in the ends. Repeat this process a further four or five times until the rose starts to look full. Use a larger petal cutter for each layer.

6 For the outer layers, cut out five petals using the largest petal cutter. Soften the edges and vein. Moisten the sides of each petal and secure around the rose, this time overlapping them. Curl back the edges using either your finger or a cocktail stick (toothpick).

7 For the final layer, repeat step 6 using the same size cutter. The rose should now be quite full and open.

COLOURING THE ROSE

8 For the colouring of the rose, mix together some pink, plum and violet petal dusts. Be quite firm in dusting the centre of the rose in order to achieve a deeper colour. Gradually lighten the colour as you get to the edges until it finally becomes quite pale.

CALYX

9 For the calyx, roll a ball of pale green flowerpaste into a cone and pinch out the base to form a hat shape. Using a small celstick, roll out the base to make it thinner. Cut out the calyx using cutter R11b and elongate each sepal by rolling with a celstick.

10 Use curved scissors to make fine cuts into the sides of a few sepals, then place onto a pad and soften the edges. Cup the inside of each sepal using the rounded end of a celstick.

11 Moisten the centre of the calyx and then attach it to the back of the rose, curling back the sepals.

12 The backs of the sepals should be dusted with moss green and the edges with plum petal dust. The fronts of the sepals are dusted with a mixture of moss green and white.

BUDS

13 For the buds, roll a ball of white flowerpaste into a cone with a sharp point. Tape the stem of a 20-gauge wire and bend the end of it into a small hook. Insert the moistened hook into the cone and secure.

14 Roll out some pale claret flowerpaste quite thinly. Cut out four petals using the smallest of the rose petal cutters and place them on a pad. Soften the edges, moisten the centre part of one of the four petals and place it against the cone, leaving at least 5mm (¼in) of the petal above the cone. Tuck the left-hand side of the petal around so that it hides the top completely. Wrap the other side around in order to form a tight spiral, but leaving the end open.

15 Moisten the bases of the remaining three petals. Tuck the first petal into the open side of the first that is on the cone. The second petal needs to go underneath the first and the third petal underneath the second. Close all the petals tightly around the cone, pulling them down at an angle.

16 You should stop and add a calyx at this point if you are planning to make a small bud.

17 If you wish to make a larger bud, you should follow step 15 but open up the last petal. Roll out some flowerpaste and cut out an extra three petals using a slightly larger cutter. Soften the edges and vein the petals. Continue as before, tucking the petals into the previous ones.

18 Once the buds are completed, follow steps 9 to 12 to create the calyces for your buds.

LEAVES

19 For the leaves, roll out some mid-green flowerpaste, leaving a thick ridge down the centre (a grooved board may be used for this). Cut out one large

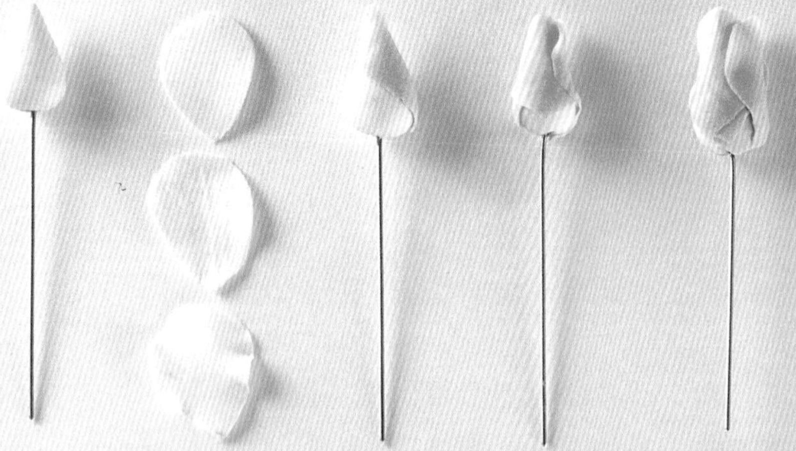

leaf, two medium and two small ones for each single stem.

20 Cut a 28-gauge wire into four equal sections. Moisten the end of each section and insert into the leaf ridge, about halfway up. Place the leaves on a pad, soften the edges and then vein. Carefully pinch out the vein down the centre.

21 Dust the back of the leaves with white petal dust mixed with a touch of moss green. The leaf fronts are dusted with moss green and the edges with plum. Dip each individual leaf into half glaze then allow them to dry.

22 Tape the leaves together in groups of either three or five. Assemble the leaves starting with the large leaf, then moving on to the medium ones and finally to the small ones.

Little Mermaid Spray

The delicate pink of the roses and the lovely silvery grey of the leaves contrast beautifully with the bluey tones of the foliage in this spray (right). The berries provide a strong counterpoint.

Flowers

3 full 'Queen of Denmark' roses

3 'Queen of Denmark' rosebuds

3 stems of sea holly (see pages 66–7)

3 stems of mahonia berries (see page 68)

7 stems of eucalyptus (see page 69)

Equipment

Nile green floristry tape

Plastic posy pick

Spiralled metal cone container

1 Start by taping the three open roses together. Add the buds one at the top of the spray and two near the bottom. Add the sea holly and the eucalyptus leaves. Curve several of the leaf stems to create some movement.Then add the mahonia berries, trimming away any excess wires as you tape so that the stem is not too thick.

2 Insert the handle into a plastic posy pick and then into the vase. Arrange the spray to your satisfaction.

CLIMBER & RAMBLER ROSES

For this cake I have combined two different miniature roses, a rambler and a climber, to create a spray with flowers that appear delicate, yet also young and lively. As such, this would make a fine cake for a christening or for a child's birthday, although with the predominance of pink it would suit a young girl. *–Tombi*

Pink Perfection

Cake and Decoration

25cm (10in) teardrop cake
Apricot glaze
1kg (2¼lb) white almond paste (marzipan)
Clear alcohol (kirsch or Cointreau)
1kg (2¼lb) white sugarpaste (cold rolled fondant)
33cm (13in) teardrop cake board
Gum tragacanth powder
500g (1lb) shell pink sugarpaste (cold rolled fondant)
Pastel pink and rosé pink petal dusts
Pink bridal satin dust
Fine pink ribbon to trim cake
Broad pink ribbon to trim board

Flowers

1 spray of 'Mme. Cécile Brünner' roses
1 spray of Ballerina roses

Equipment

Wild silk textured rolling pin (HP)
Decorative edge scissors
Flower pick

PREPARATION

1 Brush the cake with apricot glaze and cover with almond paste. Allow to dry for three days. Moisten the almond paste with clear alcohol and cover with white sugarpaste, covering the cake board at the same time. Use smoothers to achieve a good finish and a neat join between the base of the cake and the board. Allow to dry for a week.

2 Knead one teaspoon of gum tragacanth into the shell pink sugarpaste, wrap in cling film then place in a plastic bag. Allow the paste to mature overnight.

3 Roll out the gum paste and texture with the textured rolling pin. Make a template using the cake tin and then cut out a teardrop drape. Trim the edge with decorative scissors. Place the drape over the cake and arrange attractively. Do not stick the drape to the cake so that it can be removed easily before the cake is cut.

4 Dust the board and the drape with the pastel pink petal dust and pink bridal satin dust. Dust the cake below the drape with rosé pink petal dust, and dust the board again using the same colour. Fasten ribbon around the base of the cake and board. Place the flower spray in the pick and carefully insert into the cake.

BALLERINA RAMBLER

This is a delightful miniature rambling rose. The configuration is almost the same as for the dog rose, but differs in a few essentials. These roses fade quite rapidly as they age, giving the plant a variety of tones when in bloom. Seen en masse, the flowers range from dark pink to almost white. Another difference is that, being hybridized, they only have five leaves in each leaflet, while the centre differs slightly from the dog rose as well. To make this rose, follow the basic instructions for making the dog rose (see pages 12–15) and then follow the substitute steps on page 47.

'Mme. Cécile Brünner' Climber

This miniature climbing rose grew up the side of our house when I was a child, scenting the lounge with its delicate perfume. Cultivating it was a great achievement in the arid area of South Africa where we lived. In the middle of the worst droughts the rose would be carefully nurtured with our bath water, which also killed the aphids!

Materials

33-, 30-, 28-, 26-, 24-, and 20-gauge wires

Pale green and pale pink flowerpaste (gum paste)

Pastel pink, rosé pink, lemon, vine green holly/ivy and forest green petal dusts

White bridal satin dust

Quarter or half glaze

Equipment

Scalpel

Rose petal cutters (TT350, 351, 352)

Medium rose petal veiner (GI)

Dimpled foam

Calyx cutter (OP R13)

'Mme. Cécile Brünner' leaf veiners (Silicone Plastique, see p34)

Nile green floristry tape

BUDS

1 Make small, slender pointed rose cones on one-third length 20-gauge wires. Then roll out flowerpaste very finely and cut out petals with the smallest cutter. Work the edge of each petal on your foam pad using a ball tool, then moisten and wrap around the cone to create a tight bud. For some of the buds you can now add a calyx and set aside to dry.

2 For the next size of buds, cut out two petals with the medium cutter. Soften the petal edges, moisten down the lower edges and interlock two petals to form a fine, pointed bud. Gently curve back the upper edges of the petal with a metal frilling tool or cocktail stick (toothpick). Add a calyx and leave to dry.

3 To form the largest buds, cut out three petals with the medium cutter and soften the petal edges as before. Dust the petal veiner and vein each petal. Moisten the edges and spiral the three petals. Gently curve back the petals. Add a calyx and set aside to dry.

FLOWERS

4 Follow steps 1–3 to make the rose centres. Cut out five or six petals with the largest cutter, making the paste slightly thicker at the narrow end. Cut 33-gauge wire into one-fifth lengths and make a small hook at one end of the wire. Moisten the hook and insert into the thicker paste. Vein the petals. Gently cup the centre of the petals. Frill the edge of the petals and set to dry on dimpled foam.

5 Dust the top of the small buds with a mixture of the pastel and rosé pink. Give the smallest buds the deepest colour. Dust the base of the petals with lemon yellow and vine green. Dust the rose centres with pastel and rosé pink, a little paler than the buds. Dust the edge of the outer petals with pastel pink only. Tape the outer petals around the centres of the roses and arrange the petals attractively. Add the calyces.

CALYX

6 Roll a small ball of pale green paste into a cone. Flatten out the broad end so that the pedicel is fine enough to fit

into the centre of the calyx cutter. Cut out and place the calyx on the board. Then elongate each sepal, cup the centre of the calyx and cup the centre of each sepal. Cut fine hairs along the edges of the sepals with scissors. Dust the inside of the sepals with white bridal satin dust. Moisten the centre of the calyx and attach it to a bud or flower. Dust the outside of the calyces with the holly/ivy dust and then add a streak of the forest green dust up the centre of the calyx. Be careful to leave the edges of the sepals pale green.

LEAVES

7 Roll out pale green paste over a medium or small groove on a grooved board. Cut 30-gauge wires in fifths, moisten the wire and place along the groove. Roll over the wire and embed it firmly. Fold back the paste over the wire and roll out again. Remove the wire and paste and vein the leaf. Trim off the leaf just outside the markings with scissors. Use a sharp scalpel and flicking cuts to create serrations on the leaf edges. Gently soften the edge of the leaf with a dresden tool. Dust the leaves with holly/ivy dust and a little forest green. Make the underside of the leaf slightly paler. Emphasize the veining with the dust. Highlight the edges with some of the rosé. Allow to dry, then glaze. Tape the leaves into groups of seven with nile green floristry tape. Steam to set.

'BALLERINA' RAMBLER

Follow the instructions on pages 12–15 for making the Dog rose but substitute the following stages:

CENTRES

1 Wind thread 20 times around a finger. Twist into a figure of eight, thread 1½ length 30-gauge wire through the loops and twist to tighten. Trim the cotton. Dip into egg white. Separate the filaments of cotton and curve with tweezers. Allow to dry. When dry and stiff, dip the tip of the threads into egg white and dip into mimosa sugartex. Ensure it does not clump. Roll a small ball of pale green paste, moisten the centre of the stamens and fasten the green paste into place. Cut a stamen very short and insert into the centre of the green paste to form a protruding pistil. Dust this centre with a little vine green and holly/ivy petal dusts.

2 Make five very pale pink petals for each half or full flower, using heart-shaped petal cutters TT329 and 328. The heart shapes will need to be elongated. The paste at the pointed end should be thicker to allow for the insertion of a hooked, moistened 33-gauge wire. The petals on each flower are uneven in shape and size.

COLOURING

3 Dust the base of each petal lightly with lemon and vine green. Dust the petals of the half roses a deeper pink than the full roses. Some of the full roses should be dusted a little paler than the half roses, others still a paler pink. Finally, some should be dusted with edelweiss on the outside of the petals to create the faded look of the real flowers.

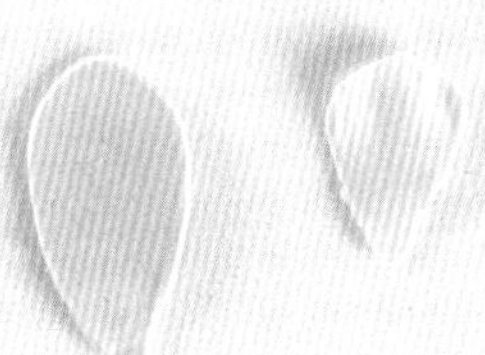
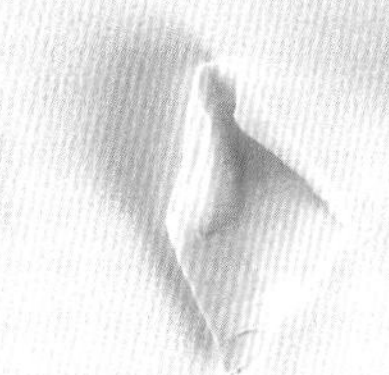

I created this unusual cake to celebrate the 70th birthday of my fellow cake decorating friend, Peter, whose favourite flowers were roses of any sort. Sadly he died before his birthday, so this cake is now a tribute to a very talented cake decorator and a wonderful human being. – *Alan*

Blue Peter Rose Cake

Cake and Decoration

15cm (6in) and 23cm (9in) octagonal cakes
Apricot glaze
1.5kg (3⅓lb) white almond paste (marzipan)
Clear alcohol (kirsch or Cointreau)
2kg (4½lb) violet sugarpaste (cold rolled fondant)
35cm (14in) octagonal board
15cm (6in) long octagonal thin board
Mauve and violet ribbons to trim cakes
Royal icing
Broad blue/violet ribbon to trim board
Violet and black food colour pens

Flowers

2 fully blown 'Blue Peter' roses
1 full 'Blue Peter' rose
12 'Blue Peter' rosebuds at various stages
11 sets of rose leaves

Equipment

Black florists' reel wire

PREPARATION

1 Brush both cakes with the apricot glaze and then cover with white almond paste. Leave the cakes to dry overnight. Moisten the surface of the almond paste with clear alcohol and cover with violet-coloured sugarpaste, using smoothers to achieve a good finish. Cover the larger board with the violet sugarpaste as well, and then transfer the base tier on top.

2 Place the small cake onto the same-sized thin board and then position on top of the base tier. Use a sugarpaste smoother to apply pressure to form a firm and neat bond between the two cakes. Allow the cakes to dry for at least a couple of days.

3 Attach two bands of thin ribbon to the base of both cakes, using a small amount of royal icing to hold them in place at the back. Glue a band of broader ribbon to the board edge using a non-toxic glue stick.

SIDE DESIGN

4 The minimalist side design for this cake is based upon some very ornate silver and black wrapping paper. I have drawn the design onto the cake freestyle using food colour pens, choosing violet and black rather than silver to fit in with the overall colour scheme of the cake. The design imitates the trailing curves of the wire tendrils in the rose spray, combining small five-petal blossom shapes that have a free-style quality, with linking stems. Practise drawing the design a little if you are not confident of your freestyle skills, and then draw it round the board, along the sides of both cakes and creeping across the top of the top tier cake.

FLOWERS

5 Wire together two sprays using the rosebuds as the leaders and the larger flowers as the focal flowers. Add black wire tendrils to create an unusual stylized display.

'Blue Peter'

This unusual miniature rose blooms throughout the summer and autumn months. The magenta-coloured buds open up to reveal a mature flower with a more lavender-purple hue, making it a versatile rose appropriate not only for ruby weddings but also on cakes for men.

Materials

Small seedhead stamens

30-, 28-, 26-, 24- and 20-gauge white wires

Pale ruby and holly/ivy flowerpaste (gum paste)

Primrose, lemon, vine green, African violet, aubergine, plum, forest green, holly/ivy, and white petal dusts

Deep magenta craft dust

Half glaze

Equipment

Australian rose petal cutters (TT349, 351)

Ceramic silk veining tool (HP)

Rose calyx cutter (OP R13)

Pointed rose leaf cutters (J)

Briar rose leaf veiner (GI)

Nile green floristry tape

STAMENS

1 Take a small group of small seedhead stamens and glue them together, starting from the centre and working up towards the tips at both ends of the stamens. Allow to set slightly, then trim to produce two small groups. Repeat the above a few times.

2 Next, glue one group of the trimmed stamens onto the end of a 24-gauge wire. You will need to squeeze the stamens firmly against the wire to fix the wire and stamens together. Apply a touch of non-toxic hi-tack glue to the next group of stamens and add them to the first set of stamens. Repeat this process until you have formed a neat centre for the rose, then leave to dry.

3 Dust the tips with primrose and lemon petal dusts and then dust the centre of the group with vine green. Curl the stamens with tweezers to make them more realistic.

PETALS

4 You will need to make approximately 20 petals for each flower. Starting with the smallest petal size, roll out some ruby-coloured paste, leaving a thick ridge for the wire.

5 Cut out a small petal shape and insert a moistened 30-gauge wire. Some of the petals can be left whole while others will need to have a V-shaped cut taken out of the overall petal shape. Vein the petal gently using the ceramic silk veining tool.

6 Soften the edges of each petal on a pad using the metal ball tool. Cup the centre of each petal. Pinch the base of the petal between your finger and thumb and then allow it to dry slightly.

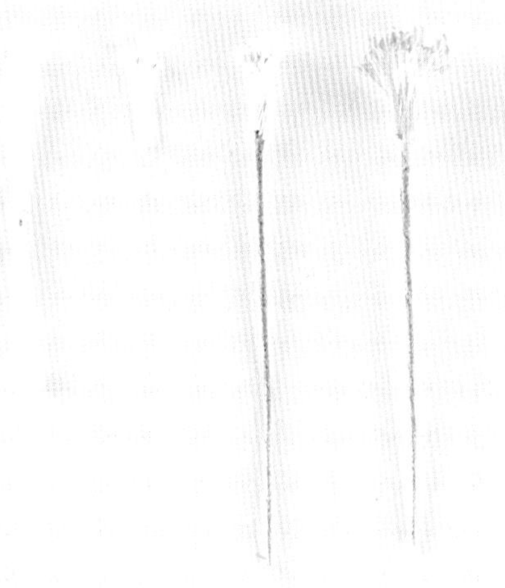

Repeat the process working through the rose petal sizes until you have made a total of 20 petals, keeping the larger sizes as a whole shape.

COLOURING AND ASSEMBLY

7 Dust each petal using a mixture of deep magenta craft dust and African violet petal dust, dusting from both the base and the edges of each petal.

8 Tape the various sizes of petals tightly around the stamens with some quarter-width nile green floristry tape, starting with the smallest V-trimmed petals and gradually working up to the larger sizes. Add a calyx as for the 'Mme. Cécile Brünner' rose (see pages 46–7).

BUDS

9 To form the buds, first of all make small, slender pointed rose cones on third-length 20-gauge wires. Next, roll out some flowerpaste very finely and, using the smallest cutter, cut out enough small petals to add one petal to each rose cone. Cover with a plastic mat.

10 Work the edge of each petal in turn on a foam pad, moisten with egg white and wrap tightly around the cone to create a tight bud. To make the centre of each bud, take two petals and curl them opposite one another to form a heart shape. For some of the buds you can now add a calyx and then set them aside to dry.

11 For the second layer, cut out two petals with the medium cutter. Soften the edges of each petal on the foam pad, moisten down the lower edges of the petal with egg white and interlock two petals to form a fine, pointed bud. Next, gently curve back the upper edges of the petal using either a metal frilling tool or a cocktail stick (toothpick). Add a calyx and set aside to dry.

12 For the third layer, cut out three petals with the medium cutter. Soften the edge of each petal on the foam pad with a metal ball tool. Dust the veining tool and vein each petal. Moisten the edges and spiral the three petals. Gently curve back the petals to achieve an attractive finish and then finally add a calyx and set to one side to dry.

LEAVES

13 Roll out some holly/ivy flowerpaste, remembering to leave a thick ridge for the wire (you might prefer to use a grooved board for this job as you will need to make quite a number of leaves). The leaves grow in sets of five. Cut out the leaf shape using one of the two smaller pointed rose leaf cutters. Insert a 30- or 28-gauge wire into the thick ridge. Soften the edges and then vein the leaves using the large briar rose leaf veiner. Pinch each leaf firmly at the tip and at the base.

14 To achieve strong green leaves, it is important to dust them before they have had time to dry fully. Dust the edges with a mixture of aubergine and plum petal dusts. Dust forest green from the base to the tip, fading the colour towards the edges. Overdust with holly/ivy and vine green. Keep the backs paler by dusting with a little of the greens and then with white petal dust.

15 Dip the leaves into a half glaze and then tape them together into sets of five. There should be a large space between the first three leaves and the two at the base.

The design for this cake combines 'Old Blush' and 'Cathedral Splendour' roses to create alternate tones of light and dark pink. When the celebration is over, the pompom can be kept as a memento of the occasion and the roses decorating the velvet board may be given to guests as favours. *–Tombi*

The Pompom Cake

Cake and Decoration

23cm (9in) round cake

Apricot glaze

850g (1¾lb) white almond paste (marzipan)

Clear alcohol (kirsch or Cointreau)

1.26kg (2¾lb) ivory sugarpaste (cold rolled fondant)

35cm (14in), 25cm (10in) and 23cm (9in) round boards

White satin ribbon to trim cake

Sage satin ribbon to trim 25cm (10in) board

Sage green velvet to cover 35cm (14in) and 23cm (9in) boards

Flowers

15 full 'Old Blush' roses

10 'Old Blush' rosebuds

6 full 'Cathedral Splendour' roses

11 'Cathedral Splendour' rosebuds

40 sets of rose leaves

Equipment

1 short spiked crystal pillar (W)

1 small celnest (C)

Nile green floristry tape

PREPARATION

1 Brush the cake with apricot glaze and then cover with almond paste. Leave the cake to dry at least overnight.

2 Moisten the surface of the almond paste with clear alcohol and cover with ivory sugarpaste. Using smoothers, smooth out the surface and sides of the cake.

3 Cover the 25cm (10in) board with some ivory sugarpaste and position the cake on top. Use sugarpaste smoothers to try to form a neat join between the cake and the board.

4 Attach a thin band of white satin ribbon to cake base with a little sugarpaste softened with clear alcohol.

5 Glue a band of sage satin ribbon onto the side edge of the 25cm (10in) board using a non-toxic glue stick.

POMPOM

6 To make the pompom topping the cake, tape three sets of rose leaves to surround a 'Cathedral Splendour' rose and then tape a further ten 'Old Blush' roses around this central spray.

7 Next, tape sprays of rose leaves to several 'Cathedral Splendour' rosebuds and then intersperse these sprays with the 'Old Blush' roses. Finish off the pompom by taping five sets of rose leaves around the base. Cut off any excess wires and then neatly tape the handle.

ASSEMBLY

8 Insert the handle of the pompom into the short spiked crystal pillar and then insert pompom and pillar into the centre of the cake.

9 Cover the 35cm (14in) and 23cm (9in) boards with sage green velvet. Gather the velvet in such a way that you create a 'rippled' effect. Having done this, place the large green velvet-covered board gathered side up.

10 Fasten the second velvet-covered board in the centre of the first to cover the gathering thread.

11 Place the celnest in the centre of the 23cm (9in) board and carefully position the cake with the completed pompom onto the celnest.

VELVET BOARD DECORATION

12 Tape together groups of 'Cathedral Splendour' roses and rosebuds with grouped sets of rose leaves.

13 Repeat this with groups of 'Old Blush' roses, rosebuds and leaves. Finish off the groups of flowers neatly and arrange them on the velvet board with alternate 'Old Blush' and 'Cathedral Splendour' sprays.

'OLD BLUSH'

The 'Old Blush' rose is a very old rose. Although it is usually grown as a bush it can, with patience, be encouraged to grow fairly tall against a supporting wall. This rose is unusual – I picked five flowers when making my samples and all had just nine petals! However hard I looked I could not find even a small, misshapen petal to make up the customary five petals to a layer.

Materials

28-, 26- and 18-gauge wires

Very pale pink, pale green and mid-green flowerpaste (gum paste)

Fine seedhead stamens

Non-toxic hi-tack glue

Lemon, brown, rosé pink, vine green, holly/ivy and forest green petal dusts

White bridal satin dust

Quarter glaze

Equipment

Standard petal templates (see page 154)

Plain-edged cutting wheel (PME)

Silk veining tool (HP)

Rose petal veiner (5.5cm) (GI)

Smooth porcelain tool (HP)

Rose calyx cutter (OP R11)

Large plastic pale green rose leaf cutter (J)

Black plastic rose leaf cutters (large and medium) (J)

Large briar rose leaf veiner (GI)

Dimpled foam

Nile green floristry tape

STAMENS

1 Cut a half-length of the 18-gauge wire and form a hook at one end of the wire. Using a small amount of pale green flowerpaste, make a small pad on the hook. Cut off enough short lengths of the fine seedhead stamens to cover the entire pad of green flowerpaste. Press these stamens into the pad. Allow to dry until firm.

2 Group together between 10 and 15 stamens and use non-toxic hi-tack glue to moisten the threads and stick them together into fairly flat groups, being careful to leave some of the filaments just below the anthers loose. Cut lengths from either end of the stamens long enough to reach the wire and taller than the stamens stuck into the pad of green paste. Moisten the wire with non-toxic hi-tack glue and stick the groups of stamens into position. Allow to dry thoroughly and then dust the stamens first with some lemon dust and then with some brown petal dust.

PETALS

3 Cut out the nine petal shapes. Place the first template over a piece of very pale pink flowerpaste, which has a thickened end. The point of the rose petal should fit over the thickened paste. Cut out the petal using the smooth cutting wheel.

4 Cut the 28-gauge wires into one-fifth lengths and then hook one end of the wires with fine-nosed pliers. Moisten the

hooked end of a wire and insert it into the thickened edge of the flowerpaste. Increase the size of wire as the petals get larger

5 Place the petals on a foam pad and soften the edges with a metal ball tool. Then place the petals between cornflour-(cornstarch-) dusted rose petal veiners and vein the petal. Work the edge of the petal gently with the silk veining tool, gently cup the petal and place on a curved apricot or apple tray to set.

6 Only use the rose petal veiner on the smallest petals. As the petals get larger they should be more strongly veined with the silk veining tool. Use a large metal ball tool to cup the larger petals. Some of the outer petals can be further enhanced by frilling the edges with a frilling tool.

7 When all nine petals have been made, allow them to set, but make sure that they are not allowed to dry out. Dust the petals with a little lemon and vine green dusts at the base of each petal. Then give them each a light dusting of rosé pink from the centre of the petal towards the edge on both the upper and lower surfaces.

CONES FOR THE BUDS

8 The cones for these particular roses should be long, narrow and at least 5mm (¼in) shorter than the smallest petal. Roll a medium piece of pale pink flowerpaste into a ball. Then roll into a long, narrow cone.

9 Cut one-third of the 18-gauge wire and form a hook at one end. Moisten the wire and push it into the base of the cone. Fasten the cone to the wire. Set aside to dry completely.

BUDS

10 Use the smallest petal template from page 154 to make the buds. Roll out the paste and cut around the template with the cutting wheel. You can use one, two or three spiralled petals to make a balanced selection of buds.

11 Soften the edges of the petals using the silk veining tool. Using the smooth porcelain tool, carefully turn back the

edges of the petals of the buds. Allow the buds to dry thoroughly.

CALYX

12 Make a cone using some pale green paste. Pinch out the thick end into a circle. Place this circle on a grooved board and roll out the paste until you reach a suitable thickness. Position the rose calyx cutter over the pedicel and cut out the shape.

13 Use a medium celstick to elongate each sepal slightly. Place the sepals on a foam pad, one after another, and mark a groove down the centre of each individual sepal using a dresden tool. This process will also encourage the sepals to curl, creating a more natural effect.

14 Use a pair of fine-bladed scissors to cut fine hairs on the edge of the sepals. Use the base of the medium celstick to make a hollow in the centre of the calyx.

15 Dust the inside of the calyx with the white bridal satin dust. Dust the centre of the outside of the sepals first with holly/ivy, then slash a streak of dark green dust up the middle, making sure you leave sepal edges pale.

16 Moisten the centre of the calyx and fasten it to the base of the dried buds. If a bud happens to have only a few petals, then the sepals can be arranged closer to these petals. Note that there is no marked hip groove on the 'Old Blush' roses or buds. Tape the stem below the calyces using half-width nile green floristry tape.

LEAVES

17 First roll out a quantity of mid-green flowerpaste. Use the large pale green plastic cutter and both the large and medium black plastic leaf cutters to cut out leaf shapes from the paste. Place them on the foam pad.

18 Soften the cut edges of the leaves with the ball tool, then vein the leaves with the large briar leaf veiner. Set the leaves on some dimpled foam and allow them to dry until they are leather hard.

19 Dust the leaves firstly with a quantity of holly/ivy green petal dust and secondly with a lighter dusting of the forest green petal dust.

20 Allow the leaves to dry out and then glaze them with a quarter glaze. Once the glaze has completely set, tape the leaves into groups of five with nile green floristry tape

ASSEMBLY

21 Starting with the smaller petals, tape all the petals around the prepared stamens to assemble the flower. 'Old Blush' roses are very irregular in shape, so you should feel free to take a 'relaxed' attitude.

22 Form calyces as described for the buds. Add them to the roses, ensuring the sepals curve downwards. Steam the completed flowers to set the dust.

'Cathedral Splendour'

This is a boldly coloured modern rose, which becomes rather untidy when fully opened. I have used it in its partially opened state when it is, I feel, at its most attractive. The back of the petals are pale pink and the upper surfaces of the petals are a bold, bright pink. The buds are sharply pointed, delicate in shape and are lightly dusted with lemon above a rosy base – the tips of the petals are curled back to show the deep pink inner petals.

Materials

- Pale pink and green flowerpaste (gum paste)
- 26- and 18-gauge wires
- Lemon, rosé pink, and vine, holly/ivy and dark green petal dusts
- Deep magenta craft dust
- White bridal satin dust
- One-third glaze

Equipment

- Fleximat
- Rose petal cutters (TT549, 550, 551)
- Very large rose petal veiner (GI)
- Smooth porcelain tool (HP)
- Nile green floristry tape
- Rose calyx cutter (TT245 or OP R11b)
- Dimpled foam
- Light green and black leaf cutters (J)
- Briar rose leaf veiner (GI)

CONE

1 Take a piece of pale pink paste and roll it into a smooth ball. Then roll it into a long, pointed cone with a broad base.

2 Moisten a half-length 18-gauge hooked wire and insert it into the base of the cone. The cone should be no longer than the smallest petal you are using to make the rose. For buds it should be at least 0.5cm (¼in) smaller than the small cutter size. Leave the cones to dry.

CENTRE

3 Cut out four petals using the smallest cutter. Place three under the fleximat while you work on the fourth petal. Place on a foam pad and soften the petal with a metal ball tool. Vein the petal strongly with the petal veiner.

4 Moisten the petal and place the cone on top. If you are making a bud, ensure that the base of the cone is covered by the petal. Roll the petal around the cone, creating a very tight spiral at the tip. You must not be able to see the cone at all. Prepare all the rose cones in this way. If you are creating a bud, the edge of the petal can be rolled back gently.

5 Next cut out three petals, soften the edges and vein strongly. Moisten each petal down the left-hand side, about three-quarters of the length from the tip. Place the prepared rose cone onto the centre of the first petal. Stick down the moistened edge.

6 Now tuck the next two petals inside one another, spiralling all three petals. Loosely spiral them around the cone. It is important to pull down on the edges of the petals to tighten the centre; at the same time these petals must be taller than the first layer. Using the smooth porcelain tool or a small celstick, roll back the side edges of the petals very gently. If you are making a bud, roll back one more strongly than the other. The next layer also has three petals, and the process is exactly the same as before.

7 Add another three petals, this time using the second-sized cutter, keeping the petals tight. If you are creating a bud, you can loosen the petals slightly at this stage, concentrating on getting a neat base to the flower and giving graceful curls to the edges of the petals.

HALF ROSE

8 To create the half rose, cut out a further three petals using the largest cutter. This time, cup the petals using a metal ball tool or simply by pressing hard into the centre of the petal with your thumb.

9 The petals are arranged over the joins of the previous layer without tucking them below the edges of the petals. Make sure that the petals are curved back strongly, giving an almost triangular look to the petal as you look at it from the top of the rose. (This is a very typical characteristic of the 'Cathedral Splendour' rose.)

10 Add a calyx at this stage to finish the half rose.

FULL ROSE

11 To form the outer, wired petals, first lighten the paste very slightly. Roll the

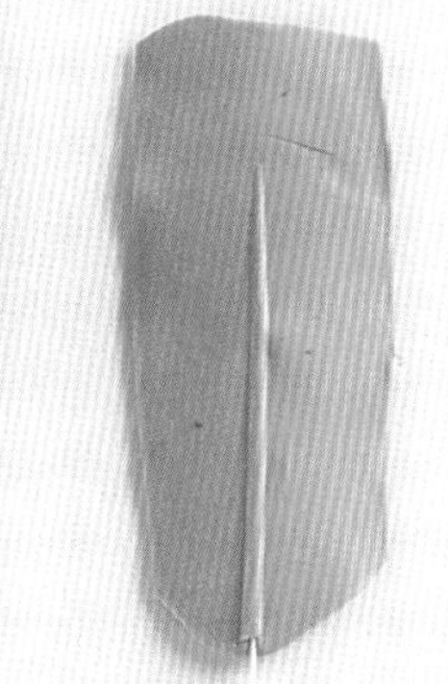

paste a little thicker at the pointed base of the petals. Cut 26-gauge wires into quarter lengths and hook one end. Moisten the wire and insert into the thickened edge of the paste. Vein the petals strongly, then gently soften the edges of the petals with a frilling tool. Cup each petal strongly and continue with the 'V'-shaping of the petals for the first three wired petals. The two outer petals can be more loosely shaped.

COLOURING THE PETALS

12 When they are set but not dry, dust the bases of the petals with a little lemon yellow dust. Just above this, dust the top surface of the petals first with a strong dusting of rosé pink and then a light overdusting of deep magenta craft dust, making the colour deepest towards the lower part of the petal. The colour should gently taper to paler edges. The backs of the petals have a rosy blush just above the dusting of lemon, but the upper parts of the backs of the petals are pale pink.

ASSEMBLING THE ROSE

13 As this rose is at its best as a bud or partially open, tape only five petals onto the half rose stage in order to make the full rose. Always make sure that you are taping tightly against the centre. Remember that the inner layer of wired petals has the more emphasized V-shape.

14 Pull down on the wires in order to bed the petals into place. A better look is usually achieved by wiring and then pulling the first three petals in place – instead of adding them to the outside of the group. Once all the petals are in place, tape over the full length of the wire with full-width floristry tape, steeply angled to give a smooth stem to your rose. This can be improved by polishing the tape with the back of a knife.

CALYX

15 Roll a piece of green paste into a ball, then into a cone and pinch out flat to leave a narrow pedicel. Place the cutter over the pedicel and cut out the calyx shape. Roll each sepal slightly longer and soften the edges. Cut the sepal edges with fine scissors. Cup each sepal and the centre of the calyx. Dust the inside of the calyx with white bridal satin dust. Run down the centre of each sepal with a dresden tool.

16 Moisten the centre of the calyx and stick in place, ensuring the sepals go over the joins between the petals. Use a small celstick to mark in the beginning of the rose hip. The rose hip is fairly slender until the stamens show in the centre of a rose. If the calyx is being attached to a bud, stick several of the sepals up against the petals (these are usually the sepals without the cuts). Arrange the other sepals attractively.

LEAVES

17 Roll out the green paste along the groove, place the moistened wire along the groove and roll it in. Fold back the paste over the wire and roll out again, place the cutter over the groove and cut out the leaf. Soften the edge of the leaf with the ball tool. Vein the leaf and set it to dry on dimpled foam. Choose the finest groove on your board so that the leaves do not have the hard 'grooved' look to the veins at the back.

18 Dust the leaves before they are dry, first with a layer of holly/ivy green and then with an overdusting of dark green. It is important to do this when the leaves are leather hard to obtain a good depth of colour. As I have used rosé pink petal dust on the petals it can also be added to the edge of the leaves to provide more interest. The leaves of this rose tend to be more shiny than most roses. Glaze the leaves with a one-third glaze. Allow the glaze to dry.

19 Tape together one large, two medium and two smaller leaves with half-width tape, taping over the short length of wire on each leaflet. Tape these onto the main stems with the buds and flowers.

MODERN ROSES

This romantic Ruby wedding cake features lovely curved lace and the delicate highlight of a tiny butterfly. I thank Doreen McCole of Chepstow for the idea of the floating lace. Cakes made for ruby wedding celebrations are often too small, and this is why I have made mine a two-tier cake. *–Tony*

Favourite Ruby Wedding

Cake and Decoration

- 15cm (6in) and 25cm (10in) oval cakes
- 35cm (14in) oval cake board
- Apricot glaze
- 2.25kg (5lb) white almond paste (marzipan)
- 2.6kg (5¾lb) shell pink sugarpaste (cold rolled fondant)
- Icing (confectioners') sugar
- Clear alcohol (kirsch or Cointreau)
- 15cm (6in) thin cake board
- 120g (4oz) flowerpaste (gum paste)
- Cornflour (cornstarch)
- 1.5m (1¾yd) burgundy 3mm (1/10in) ribbon (for the cakes)
- Pink feather-edged 9mm (⅓in) ribbon (for the board)
- Royal icing
- Plum and African violet petal dusts

Flowers

- 1 full 'Pink Favourite' rose
- 1 three-quarters 'Pink Favourite' rose
- 4 half 'Pink Favourite' roses
- 5 'Pink Favourite' rosebuds
- 4 sprigs sea holly
- 6 clusters of mahonia berries
- 7 sprays of eucalyptus leaves

Equipment

- Lace cutter (DL)
- 1cm (½in) tube for drying lace in a curve
- Oval perspex separator plate 2cm (¾in) deep and 10cm (4in) long
- Miniature butterfly cutter (DH134)
- No. 1 piping tube (tip) for the royal icing
- Nile green floristry tape
- Double-sided tape
- Flower pick

1 Brush both cakes with apricot glaze and then cover them with almond paste. Set aside to dry overnight. Roll out the shell pink sugarpaste on icing sugar. Moisten the surface of the almond paste with clear alcohol and cover with the sugarpaste. Use the smoothers to ensure a smooth coating. Sugarpaste the cake board at the same time as covering the cakes. Place the small cake on its board. Polish the surface of each cake with a smoothed handful of sugarpaste. Set aside to dry for a few days.

Lace

2 To make the lace pieces, first stiffen some flowerpaste with cornflour, then cut out lace pieces. A dab of white vegetable fat on the corner of your board will help remove the lace from the cutter by creating a slight suction. Now place the lace pieces over the tube to dry. Dry a larger number of lace pieces flat as they stand proud around the base of the cake. Use the same method to make the miniature butterfly.

3 Measure the depth of the lace, allowing a further 2.5mm (⅛in). Mark this measurement around the base of the small cake with a pair of dividers. Place the separator on the larger cake, slightly off centre. Use a small piece of non-slip matting on top of this to prevent the small cake from slipping during transport.

4 Attach the lace ribbon to the cake and cake board with a little royal icing, joining it neatly at the back. Carefully mark the line the lace will follow on the board, starting against the cake and gently spiralling out. Leave an 8cm (3in) gap towards one end to accommodate a small spray. Attach the ribbon to the board using double-sided tape.

5 Carefully dust the tips of the lace still on the tube with a mixture of the plum and African violet dusts. Dust the tips of the flat lace pieces as well. Pipe out a little royal icing to fasten the lace to the small cake just below the ribbon. Position the large cake on the cake board. Attach the ribbon to the base of the large cake, lace pieces to the board and fasten the butterfly to the cake with royal icing.

Assembly

6 Tape together rosebuds, eucalyptus leaves, mahonia berries and sea holly to make three groups. Tape these around the base of the large rose. Add the half roses and extra eucalyptus and mahonia berries to finish off. Insert the spray into a flower pick and insert this at an angle into the larger cake.

For the smaller spray, tape together eucalyptus, mahonia berries and sea holly with a rosebud. Add a half rose and an additional spray of mahonia berries with a three-quarters open rose. Place this spray in the gap on the board

'PINK FAVOURITE'

This deep pink hybrid Tea Rose originally hails from the USA but was introduced into Britain during the 1950s. The 'Pink Favourite' rose is very large and luxuriant with a sweet fragrance, and the leaves are unusually long, shiny and light green in colour.

Materials

Cyclamen and mid-green flowerpaste (gum paste)

Ruby, plum, African violet, and holly/ivy petal dusts

White bridal satin dusts

26- and 18-gauge white wires

Equipment

Rose petal cutters (TT276, 277, 150, 151)

Very large rose veiner (GI)

Calyx cutter (OP R11b)

Apple tray

Nile green floristry tape

Curved scissors

CONES

1 Roll out a ball of flowerpaste to make a rounded cone. Make sure the cone comes to a sharp point that will fit within the smallest cutter.

2 Bend a large open hook in the end of an 18-gauge wire using a pair of pliers. Moisten the end of the wire and insert it into the base of the cone. Set aside to dry. It is imperative that the cones are dry before attempting to make the rose.

PETALS

3 Roll out the cyclamen flowerpaste fairly thinly. Cut out four petals using the smallest cutter. Place the petals onto a pad and soften the edges. Vein each petal with the large rose petal veiner. Moisten the first petal with fresh egg white and wrap it around the cone. The petal should rest slightly higher than the tip of the cone and must be fastened on tightly so the cone cannot be seen.

4 Moisten a further three petals and then spiral them around the petal already in place. This is most easily done by placing the join of the first petal to the centre of the first petal on the cone, tucking each petal underneath the one before it. Ensure you have a tight centre by pulling down on the edge of the petals. At this point it is possible to form a rosebud by adding a calyx to the rose.

5 To make the next layer of petals, roll out some more of the cyclamen flowerpaste and then cut out a number of petals, remembering to increase the size of the cutter. It is best to work on three petals at a time. Soften the edge of each petal using the end of a celpin on your foam pad. Vein each petal and cup using the end of the celpin again on the foam pad.

6 Moisten the points of the petals and spiral them around the first layer, arranging the petals so that the joins of the first layer are centred in the middle of this second layer.

7 Gently curl back the edges of the petals, creating a point at the tip. It is at this point that you may add a calyx to form a half rose.

8 Increase the size of the petals once again, cutting out five petals for each rose. Soften the edges of the petals with a celpin, vein them and then fasten five petals around the cone. Again, curl back the edges of the petals. At this point you may add a calyx to form a three-quarters rose.

9 Increase the size of petal cutter. This time the paste will need to be rolled out in a sausage, leaving a thickened piece of paste at one side. Cut out five more petals, this time positioning the point over the thickened end of the paste.

10 Hook quarter lengths of 26-gauge wires, moisten and insert them into the thickened piece of paste. Place on the foam pad and soften the edges, vein the petals and cup more than for the previous layer. Place the wired petals in apple trays to set slightly.

11 Dust the petals, using a mixture of ruby, African violet and plum. Start dusting the centre of the rose, building up the colour and working towards the outer petals. The centre of the rose is very dark in colour. Dust the wired petals as well.

12 Tape the wired petals around the rose, creating a natural look to the rose. Steam the rose to set the dust. If you touch the petals when they are still damp you will spoil the colouring when adding the calyces.

CALYX

13 Take a medium ball of green flowerpaste and roll into a cone shape, then pinch out the broad end into a circle. Place the cones on your board and roll out the paste thinly using a celpin.

14 Place the cutter over the pedicel and cut out the shape. Elongate each sepal slightly.

15 Place the calyx onto a foam pad and soften the edge of each of the sepals with the back of the celpin. Carefully cut indentations into the sides of some of the sepals using curved scissors.

16 Cup the sepals with a medium celpin. Dust the inside of the calyx with the white bridal satin dust and the outside with the holly/ivy green dust. Leave a paler edge around the sides of the sepals.

17 Moisten the calyx centre and attach it to the base of the rose, alternating the sepals over the joins of the petals. Finally, curve the sepals back on the open rose, and then attach most of the sepals against the buds, leaving some to curve down.

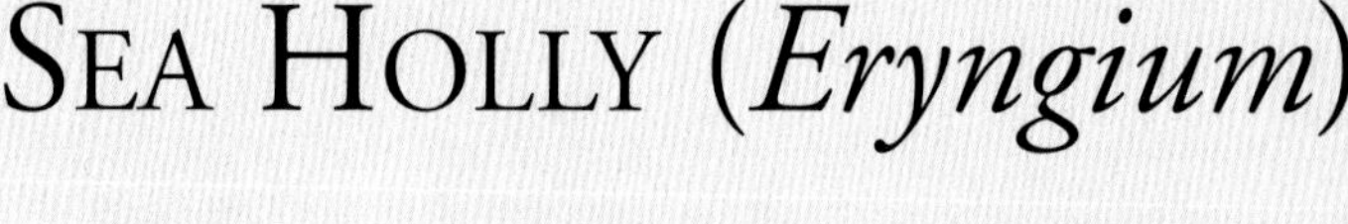

SEA HOLLY (*Eryngium*)

Sea holly is a striking plant, ideal for flower arrangers with its unusual, silvery steel-blue, spiny bracts. There are over 230 species of sea holly around the world and I have based my design on an alpine variety known as 'Amethyst'.

Materials

- Fresh stem of sea holly
- Silicone Plastique (see also page 34)
- Eucalyptus flowerpaste (gum paste)
- 28- and 20-gauge white wires
- Fine fishing line
- Deep purple, eucalyptus, white, plum, moss green and thrift petal dusts
- Isopropyl alcohol
- Silver metallic and white satin lustres

Equipment

- Scriber
- Bracts templates (see page 154)
- Plain-edged cutting wheel (PME)
- No. 00 fine paintbrush
- Double-sided rose leaf veiner
- Angled tweezers
- Thistle leaf cutter (CS)
- Nile green floristry tape

MAKING THE MOULD

1 The first step is to go out and purchase a fresh stem of sea holly, which should be readily available from any good florist shop. Next make a mould of the sea holly with the Silicone Plastique by pushing small pieces of silicone into the head of the fresh sea holly and working it in all over. Then cover the entire plant with another thin layer of the silicone, taking special care not to spread it over too thickly. Once the silicone has fully dried out, you can remove the sea holly. The mould is now ready to use.

2 Press the eucalyptus flowerpaste into the mould, small pieces at a time, using a ball tool to ensure that it gets into every space.

3 Heat a 20-gauge uncovered wire over a naked flame (a cigarette lighter or night light is best) and push it into the flowerpaste in the mould. Be careful not to push it in too far as it may cause the mould to burn.

4 Put the mould into a freezer for about half an hour to harden.

5 When ready, gently ease the head from the mould.

STAMENS

6 Using a scriber, make a small hole in each of the little heads on the sea holly and insert a small piece of fishing line into each of the heads. These will form the stamens. Leave to dry before trimming the stamens. If you try to do this too soon the pieces of fishing line are liable to come out, so be patient!

7 Once the stamens have been trimmed, dust the entire head with both the deep purple and eucalyptus petal dusts.

8 Add a small amount of isopropyl alcohol with some white petal dust and paint the bases of the stamens. Then repeat the same process with some plum petal dust and paint a small dot on top of the white.

BRACTS

9 Using the bract template on page 154, roll out a piece of flowerpaste and cut out strips using the plain-edged cutting wheel.

10 Soften the edges and cut little spines down each side. The jagged edges of the bract template are only for guidance, make sure the finished spines are much more wispy, as shown above. Paint a thin white line up the centre and then an even thinner line of the plum-coloured dust on top of the white line.

11 Dust the main section with deep purple and eucalyptus petal dusts and the base with silver metallic lustre. You will need approximately twelve bracts for each head.

12 Repeat as before using the larger template but do not colour these yet.

13 Roll a thin sausage of flowerpaste onto one end of a 28-gauge white wire and then place onto the bottom half of the double-sided veiner.

14 Place a larger bract on top of the wire, then put the top half of the veiner on top. Press together. Remove from the veiner, soften the edges and cut little spines down both sides. Make about 15 to 20 of these. Leave to dry.

15 Dust with holly/ivy green petal dust. Paint a thin white line up the centre of each of the bracts, then a thinner line of the thrift colour on top. Dust the base with silver metallic lustre.

16 Mix a small amount of flowerpaste with fresh egg white to produce a glue.

17 Brush the underside of the head with the paste and egg white glue, then attach the smaller bracts around the base. Allow to dry.

18 Tape the large bracts to the stem with nile green floristry tape.

LEAVES

19 The leaves start growing just beneath the sea holly heads, and also where a cluster of heads meets a stem approximately 8cm (3in) below the head.

20 Roll out some eucalyptus flowerpaste, leaving a ridge down the centre thick enough to accommodate a length of 28-gauge wire. Cut out the leaves from the paste using the thistle cutter. Cut a 28-gauge wire into quarter-lengths and moisten the end. Then insert the end of the wire into the ridge making sure it goes about half way up.

21 Place the leaf on a foam pad and soften the edges with the rounded end of a celpin. Pinch a vein down the centre to form a ridge. Flute the edges with a dresden tool. Dust with eucalyptus and white satin lustre.

ASSEMBLY

22 To construct the spray, tape together three stems of the head and bracts using nile green floristry tape. Then add the leaves approximately 8cm (3in) down the stem.

Mahonia Berries

These berries are poetically striking with their dark silver-blue tinge and reddish-brown stems. Discreet and unusual, they make ideal berries for sprays and arrangements.

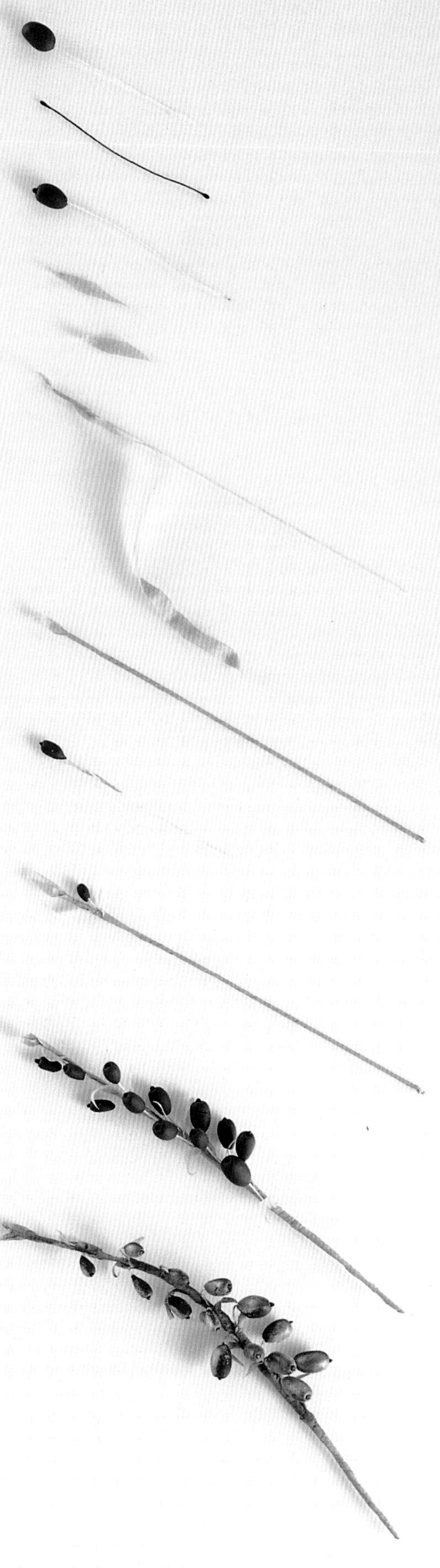

1 Cut the 30-gauge wires into lengths of five. Bend a hook into the end of each short length using a pair of fine-nosed pliers. Knead some blackberry flowerpaste until very pliable and then roll it out into small balls.

2 Moisten the hooked ends of the wire with a little fresh egg white and carefully insert the wire into the paste. Now roll the ball into more of a barrel shape. Insert a cut-off black stamen into the tip of each berry.

3 Tape around each wire with half-width beige floristry tape.

4 The berries should increase in size as they go down the stem.

5 Cutting one edge of the tape (this will create thorns as the tape is bound down the stem), tape the berries first onto 28-gauge wires. Then to form clusters of the berries tape these onto 24-gauge wires.

6 Dust the stems with a light brushing of skintone and the berries themselves with the white bridal satin dust to create the downy look.

Materials

30-, 28- and 24-gauge white wires

Blackberry flowerpaste (gum paste)

Round black stamens

Skintone and white bridal satin petal dusts

Equipment

Fine-nosed pliers

Beige floristry tape

Eucalyptus Leaves

There are many varieties of eucalyptus with different shaped leaves, from long pointed leaves to almost symmetrical. They add a soft touch of green to sprays.

Materials

28- and 20-gauge white wires

Pale eucalyptus flowerpaste (gum paste)

Silicone Plastique

Cornflour (cornstarch)

Eucalyptus, moss, plum and silver satin petal dusts

Equipment

Eucalyptus veiner made from Silicone Plastique (see page 34 for instructions)

Bougainvillaea cutters (J)

Fleximat

Dimpled foam

Beige floristry tape

METHOD

1 Cut half-width tape into half for about 2.5cm (1in). Tape to the end of a 20-gauge white wire. Twist the tape to form tiny protrusions. Cut off the excess.

2 Roll out the paste, leaving a thickened ridge. Cut out the leaves in pairs. Place them under a Fleximat.

3 Hook and moisten the end of a 28-gauge wire. Insert the wire into the base of the leaf.

4 Place the leaves on a foam pad, softening the edge with the back of a celpin.

5 Place in the cornflour-dusted veiners, vein the leaves, then place them on dimpled foam to set. While the leaves are still leather hard, dust with the eucalyptus, touch with moss green in places and blush with the plum. Overdust with the silver satin dust.

6 Steam to set the dust. If the sheen is lost then overdust once again with the silver satin petal dust.

7 Tape the leaves in pairs along the length of the 20-gauge wire, increasing the gaps between the leaves as you go down the wire.

8 Dust the stems of the spray to tone with the leaves.

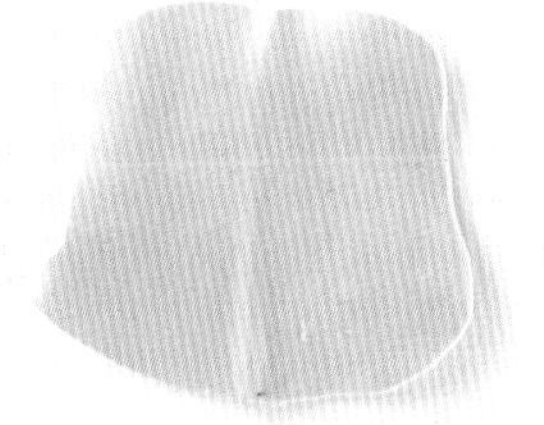

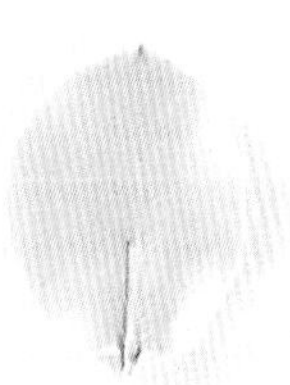
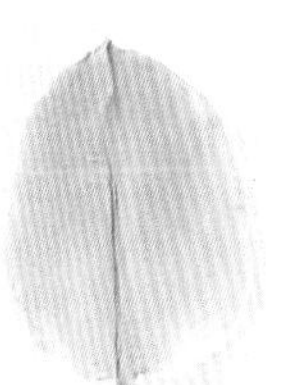

This Diamond wedding cake has been designed to extend the rose theme to a more traditional cake arrangement. The delicate lace is complemented by a stylish rosebud design on the collar. The roses have been chosen for their highly appropriate name, 'Diamond Jubilee', and their obvious beauty. – *Tony*

Diamond Jubilee

Cake and Decoration

15cm (6in), 20cm (8in) and 25cm (10in) diamond cakes

20cm (8in) and 35cm (14in) diamond cake boards

Apricot glaze

3.25kg (7lb) white almond paste (marzipan)

2kg (4½lb) pale melon royal icing

Ivory ribbon to trim boards

Cornish cream, lemon, rosé pink, moss green, white and primrose petal dusts

Clear alcohol (kirsch or Cointreau)

Flowers

5 full 'Diamond Jubilee' roses

5 half 'Diamond Jubilee' roses

9 'Diamond Jubilee' rosebuds

9 stems of ivy

Equipment

Nos. 2, 1, and 0 piping tubes (tips)

Nos. 2, 1 and 0 paintbrushes

Collar, rose runout and lace design templates (see page 152)

Small tilting perspex stand

Card and A4 plastic file pocket

PREPARATION

1 Using the cake tin, copy the diamond shape of the 20cm (8in) cake on to greaseproof (parchment) paper. It needs to be just under 1cm (½in) larger than the cake.

2 Attach the 15cm (6in) and 25cm (10in) cakes to their boards using some royal icing. The 20cm (8in) cake can be placed on a larger piece of greaseproof paper for covering with almond paste and pale melon royal icing.

3 Brush the cakes with apricot glaze then cover the tops only with almond paste. For each cake cut out four strips of almond paste and attach them to the sides. Make sure the corners are sharp. Leave to dry thoroughly.

4 Coat the tops of the cakes and then the sides with at least three layers of royal icing, allowing time between coats for the icing to dry. Try to get a smooth finish and make sure the corners are kept sharp. Coat the boards with icing as well, then leave to dry thoroughly.

5 Carefully place the 20cm (8in) cake on to the diamond-shaped greaseproof paper and cut away any excess. There must not be any paper showing. Place the cake centrally on top of the 25cm (10in) cake using a little royal icing to secure it. Pipe a fine snail trail design around the base of each cake using royal icing and a piping bag fitted with a No. 1 tube. Use double-sided tape to secure a length of ivory ribbon to the board edges.

SIDE AND TOP DESIGN

6 Trace the side and top design (see page 152) onto a piece of tracing paper. Cut a piece of card to fit into an A4 plastic file pocket and place this and the tracing paper inside so that the design shows through. Using a No. 1 tube, outline the design onto the file pocket. With a No. 1 or 2 tube and runout consistency royal icing, flood in

small sections at a time, allowing each section to dry before filling in the adjacent sections. Leave to dry.

7 Mix some alcohol with some cornish cream and lemon petal dust, then paint the roses. The edges should be painted with rose petal dust. Paint the calyces and leaves with moss green dust that has a little white added. Allow to dry.

8 Use royal icing to secure the rose design to the top of the small cake and the rosebuds to the sides of the middle cake and the board of the bottom cake.

COLLAR

9 Trace the collar design (see page 152) onto a piece of tracing paper. Place it onto a large board and cover with a suitably sized piece of waxed paper or plastic film. Secure with masking tape at each corner. Pipe the outline using melon-coloured royal icing and a piping bag fitted with a No. 1 tube.

10 Fill another piping bag with melon-coloured runout royal icing but without the tube. Cut off the end of the bag to approximately a No. 2 size hole. Following the diagram on page 152, first flood the section from A to B, then A to D, B to C and finally D to C. This method will ensure the icing will not crust over before merging at the end.

11 Now flood the rosebuds and allow each section to dry before filling in the adjacent sections. Leave to dry completely for two to three days.

12 Paint the rosebuds as described in step 7.

13 Remove the collar from the wax paper or plastic film and secure to the top of the bottom tier. Be very careful not to damage the calyces, as they are very fragile.

LACE DESIGN

14 Trace the diamond lace design from page 152 several times onto a piece of tracing paper. Using the file pocket from the side and top design, insert the lace design. Pipe over using melon royal icing and a piping bag fitted with a No. 0 tube. Allow to dry.

15 Use royal icing to attach the lace pieces to the top edge of the small cake.

ASSEMBLY

16 Place the tilting stand centrally on top of the cake.

17 Tape the flowers together in three sections, covering the two sides and back. They are arranged around the stand before the cake is placed on top. There should be a bud in the centre directly under the point of the cake with two open roses either side. Fill in the sides and back with the half roses, rosebuds and the ivy, which should extend up the sides. Try to balance them so that you have the same roses and buds either side. You are aiming almost to cover the surface of the middle tier and provide a frame around the top cake.

18 Try to arrange the flowers to your satisfaction before the cake is placed on the stand as the lace may get damaged. When you are happy with the arrangement, place the cake on the stand, being especially careful not to touch the lace.

Opposite: This driftwood arrangement shows an alternative means of displaying these beautiful roses.

'Diamond Jubilee'

'Diamond Jubilee' is a hybrid Tea Rose which originated in the USA. The buds are the least attractive feature of this glorious rose. This large, showy and abundantly petalled honey-coloured rose is highly scented. These characteristics make it highly suitable for a cake decoration. An arrangement of real flowers would provide the appropriate scent.

Materials

- Pale melon and mid-green flowerpaste (gum paste)
- 26-, 24- and 18-gauge wires
- Primrose, white, lemon, plum, moss green and aubergine petal dusts
- Myrtle lustre colour (SK)

Equipment

- Rose petal templates (page 152)
- Very large rose petal veiner (GI)
- Rose calyx cutter (OP R11B)
- Dimpled foam
- Curved scissors
- Sharp scalpel or plain-edged cutting wheel (PME)
- Nile green and beige floristry tape

CONE

1 Roll out a ball of pale melon flowerpaste into a cone with a fairly broad base. It should be no larger than the smaller rose petal template.

2 Bend an open hook at the end of an 18-gauge wire and moisten with egg white. Insert into the base of the cone, secure and allow to dry.

FIRST AND SECOND LAYERS

3 Thinly roll out a piece of pale melon flowerpaste and cut out four petals using the smaller of the rose petal templates and a sharp scalpel or plain-edged cutting wheel.

4 Place the petals on a foam pad and soften the edges using the rounded end of a large celstick. Vein each petal using the double-sided rose petal veiner.

5 Moisten the central part of one of the petals with egg white and place it against the cone. Wrap one side around to hide the cone and the other around it to form a tight spiral, leaving the end slightly open.

6 Moisten the bases of the remaining three petals. Tuck the first of the petals underneath the open end of the petal on the cone, the second one under the first and the third under the second to form an even spiral.

THIRD LAYER

7 Roll out some more paste and cut out another three petals using the middle-sized template.

8 Place the petals on a foam pad, soften the edge with the rounded end of a celstick and then vein as before.

9 Moisten the bases of each petal and tuck the first one underneath the last petal of the second layer.

10 Continue around the rose like this to form a loose even spiral. Add a calyx at this stage to form a half rose.

FOURTH LAYER

11 Cut out another three petals using the larger of the rose templates. Once again, soften and vein each of the petals with the appropriate tools, then moisten and add to the previous layer of petals.

FIFTH LAYER

12 Roll out some more melon flowerpaste to form petals for the fifth layer. These petals are wired so when rolling out the paste leave a band of thickened paste.

13 Position the point of the template over the thickened paste. Moisten hooked quarter-length 26-gauge wires and insert into the thickened piece of paste. Pinch to fasten securely.

14 Soften and vein as before. Cup the centre of each petal with your thumb and curl back the edges of the petals naturally and leave to dry over the dimpled foam.

COLOURING AND ASSEMBLY

15 Mix together some primrose and white petal dusts and colour the centre of each petal.

16 Now mix some lemon and white petal dusts and colour the outer edge of each petal. Dust the outer petals so that they are slightly paler than the inner ones.

17 Colour the centre of the wired petals with primrose and a little white petal dust. Accentuate the edges of these with a little pale plum dust.

18 Tape the wired petals around the outside of the rose using half-width nile green floristry tape, overlapping as before.

CALYX

19 For the calyx roll a ball of mid-green flowerpaste into a cone and pinch out the base to form a hat shape. Use a celstick to roll the calyx out thinner.

20 Cut out the calyx and elongate each of the sepals by rolling them out with the celstick.

21 Place the calyx on a pad and soften the edges, then cup the inner part of each sepal using the rounded end of a large celstick.

22 Use curved scissors to make some fine cuts down the edges of some of the sepals. Leave some of them uncut. Dust the inside of the whole calyx with the myrtle lustre dust.

BUDS

23 Bend an open hook at the end of an 18-gauge wire. Moisten and insert into the base of the cone and secure. Allow to dry.

24 Attach the petals to the cone following steps 5 and 6.

25 Pinch the sides of each of the petals with your finger and thumb to make bumps down the sides. This should make a very rough-looking bud, which is how they should be!

26 Mix together some primrose and white petal dust and colour the centre and the top edges of the bud. The base can be dusted with moss green. The bumps on the buds should be dusted with pale plum to highlight them.

27 Follow steps 19–22 for the calyx.

Ivy

Ivy makes an ideal trailing stem for wedding cakes, especially for winter-themed cakes since the ivy is a traditional decoration in houses at festive celebrations during the winter months; this dates back to the Druids who used it as part of their religious rituals.

Materials

Pale green flowerpaste (gum paste)

28-, 26- and 20-gauge wires

Moss green, chestnut, brown and holly/ivy petal dusts

Half glaze

Equipment

Ivy cutter (CC)

Protruding ivy leaf veiner (GI)

Fleximat

Dimpled foam

Beige floristry tape

1 Roll out some pale green flowerpaste so that a thicker ridge of paste is left down what will be the centre of the ivy leaf. Cut out ivy leaves using the cutter and place them under a Fleximat.

2 Cut the wires into quarter lengths. Moisten the end of a wire and insert it into the thickened ridge of paste. Place the leaf on a foam pad and use the back of a celpin to soften the edge of the leaf.

3 Vein the leaf in the double-sided veiner. Place the leaf on dimpled foam. Repeat for each leaf, varying the gauge of wire according to size.

4 Before the leaves are dry, but are holding their shape, dust first with moss green dust and then overdust with the chestnut to highlight the veins. Overdust with holly/ivy green to blend. Leave to dry. Glaze the leaves with half glaze.

ADDING THE LEAVES

5 Tape the leaf stems with the beige floristry tape. Start taping the 20-gauge wire with the half-width beige tape, leaving about 2.5cm (1in) of tape protruding in front of the wire. Tape down between 0.5 and 1cm (¼ to ½in). Twist the protruding tape to form a tendril, curling attractively.

6 Add the first of the small leaves, allowing about 1cm (½in) of stem leading to the main stem. Continue adding more, alternately. As the leaves get larger the spaces between them increase, as does stem length.

The spectacular 'Painter' rose, with its striped orange and cream markings, is arranged in a clear vase (below) to show off the red stems, and is combined with the 'Diamond Jubilee' rose in a hand-tied bouquet (right). The mechanics were disguised with raffia and the posy was fastened into the pot with staysoft. *– Tony*

'Painter' Rose Displays

Flowers

Terracotta Pot

5 full 'Diamond Jubilee' roses

3 'Diamond Jubilee' rosebuds (see pages 74–6)

5 full 'Painter' roses

3 'Painter' rosebuds

Clear vase

8 full and 3 half 'Painter' roses

6 'Painter' rosebuds

5 stems of rose leaves

Materials and Equipment

Terracotta pot

Clear vase

Raffia

Florists' staysoft

Nile green floristry tape

TERRACOTTA POT

1 Ensure the stems of the roses and buds are the same length. Gather the roses and buds in your left hand. Tape around the stems about a hand's breadth from the underside of the roses.

2 Tie a raffia bow over the tape to disguise it. Push staysoft into the terracotta pot and push the stems firmly into the staysoft.

CLEAR VASE

3 Arrange the roses and rosebuds in the vase so that the buds and the half roses are centrally positioned. Place leaf stems evenly around the edges in an attractive way to finish.

'PAINTER'

This is a most unusual and spectacular Floribunda rose. The petals are striped and flecked with orange and cream markings, each one strikingly different. The buds range from very dark orange to red, while the foliage is a very deep tone of green and the veins on both the leaves and roses are red. The calyces are unusual in that they have seven sepals instead of the normal five. The stems of this rose are quite spectacular, being a gorgeous, rich red.

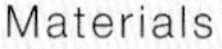

Materials

White, egg yellow, pale green and mid-green flowerpaste (gum paste)

26-, 24- and 18-gauge wires

Red, apricot, tangerine, moss green, lemon and white petal dusts

Isopropyl alcohol

White edible bridal satin lustre (SK)

Half glaze

Equipment

Rose petal cutters (TT276, 278, 550 and 551)

Very large cupped rose petal veiner (GI)

Flat, stiff brush

Small paintbrush no. 0

Rose calyx cutters (OP R11, R11b and R11c)

Extra large leaf template (see page 153)

Silicone Plastique rose leaf veiner (see page 34)

Red floristry tape

PREPARATION

1 Roll a ball of white flowerpaste into a cone with a sharp point, measuring no longer than the smallest rose petal cutter. Using an 18-gauge wire, bend an open hook into the end, moisten and insert it into the base of the cone, making sure it is firmly secured.

2 For the first and second layers, roll out egg yellow paste and cut out two petals using rose petal cutter 276. Place the petals on a foam pad and soften the edges using the rounded end of a large

celstick. Vein each petal using the petal veiner. Moisten the central part of the first petal with egg white and place it against the cone with about 5mm (¼in) of the petal above the tip of the cone. Wrap the petal around the cone so that the tip is completely hidden. Wrap the second petal around the opposite side from the first, leaving one side slightly open.

3 Roll out some more flowerpaste and cut out two further petals with the same sized cutter as before. Vein and soften the edges. Moisten the centre

and base of each petal, then tuck the first petal into the last and secure it around the back of the rose. For the second petal, repeat as before only opening it up slightly.

4 Roll out more flowerpaste, cut out two more petals with the slightly larger petal cutter. Vein and soften the edges. Cup the lower centre of each petal with the rounded end of a large celstick. Moisten the base of each petal. Place the first to one side of the rose and the second to the opposite side. Leave the front of the rose open. Curl back the edges using a cocktail stick (toothpick).

5 Cut out three more petals using a slightly larger cutter and repeat as before, attaching the petals around the rose in a spiral and leaving the ends open. Curl the petals back as before. Finally, use the largest cutter to cut out a further three petals as before.

COLOURING

6 The most striking feature of these roses is their colouring and it is a pleasure to recreate. Mix together a little red petal dust with isopropyl alcohol and lightly flick the paint onto the petals by first bending back the bristles of a flat, stiff brush and then letting go.

7 With the small No. 0 brush, paint stripes down the petals. Keep the strokes thin and light and take care that they do not turn out too uniformly spaced. Repeat the same process for the back of the petals.

8 Mix some apricot with a little red and tangerine dust and apply it to the rose centre. Lightly dust the edges of each petal, drawing the brush down from the edge to the base.

CALYX

9 Roll out a ball of pale green flowerpaste into a cone and pinch out the base so that you form a hat shape. Then thin out the base by rolling it with a celstick. Use calyx cutter R11c to cut out the shape of the calyx and then elongate each of the sepals by rolling out the paste with a celstick.

10 Roll out more flowerpaste and cut out another calyx. Cut off two of the sepals and elongate each one. Place them and the other calyx on the pad and cup the centre of each sepal. With some fine scissors, finely cut down the sides of three or four of the sepals. Moisten the back of the two separate sepals and place on the front of the calyx in between two main sepals. Dust the inner calyx with white bridal lustre, the backs with moss green petal dust and the edges with red dust.

11 Moisten the centre of the calyx and secure it to the back of the rose. Curl back the sepals on the fully blown rose to reveal the silvery colour. Finally, tape round the stem of the rose with red floristry tape. For the larger buds, follow the instructions up to step 3 but, for a tighter bud, wrap the petals further round the cone.

12 Paint the buds with red petal dust mixed with clear alcohol, but be sure to leave slight specks of the orange showing through. For bud calyces, follow the steps as before but using the cutter R11b. Attach the calyx to the

back of the bud, curling back only two or three sepals. Tape the stem with red floristry tape. Small buds have only two petals, painted deep red and wrapped tightly around a smaller cone. Cut out with calyx cutter R11 and follow the steps as before, wrapping the calyx tightly around the bud.

LEAVES

13 Roll out a quantity of mid-green flowerpaste with a ridge down the centre. You could use a grooved board for this. Cut out one large, two medium and two small leaves for each stem using the template on page 153.

14 Use the 24-gauge white wire for large leaves and the 26-gauge wire for smaller leaves. Moisten the end of the wire and insert it into the thick ridge of the leaf about halfway down.

15 Next, place the leaves on the foam pad and soften the edges with a large celstick. Vein them using the Silicone Plastique veiner. Place them on a foam sponge to allow them to dry.

16 Dilute some red petal dust with clear alcohol and paint the centre of each leaf using a fine, flat brush.

17 Mix some lemon dust with a little white petal dust and colour from the base of the wire up the side of each of the leaves. Then use some moss green petal dust to colour from the edges towards the centre. Dust the back of the leaves with moss green and white dusts.

18 Dip the leaves into half glaze and allow them to dry. Tape the leaves five to a stem with red floristry tape, starting with the largest leaves.

This two-tier cake was created to celebrate my sister Susan's wedding. The colour scheme was chosen to compliment the bridesmaid dresses which were silver grey material. The flowers used on the cake are 'Delilah' roses, small arum lilies, tradescantia leaves and silver seedheads. *–Alan*

SUSAN'S WEDDING CAKE

Cake and Decoration

20cm (8in) and 30cm (12in) teardrop cakes

2kg (4½lb) white almond paste (marzipan)

1.5kg (3⅓lb) white sugarpaste mixed with 1.5kg (3lb) champagne sugarpaste (cold rolled fondant)

Clear alcohol (kirsch or Cointreau)

38cm (15in) teardrop perspex board

Off-white royal icing

Silver-grey lustre dust

3mm rosy mauve satin ribbon to trim cakes

Pink and grey organza-type ribbons

15 paper balls

20- or 18-gauge wire

Flowerpaste (gum paste)

Silver spray

Plum, aubergine and African violet petal dusts

Flowers

2 full 'Delilah' roses

7 half 'Delilah' roses

6 'Delilah' rosebuds

14 stems of trailing tradescantia leaves

9 arum lilies

Equipment

Tilting perspex stand (with glass-headed pins)

No. 0 piping tube (tips)

White florists' staysoft

Small oval plastic plaque

Candleholder

Wire

Non-toxic hi-tack glue

PREPARATION

1 Cover the two cakes with almond paste first, then with the mixture of white and champagne sugarpaste using clear alcohol for adherence. Allow the sugarpaste to dry thoroughly. Transfer the base tier onto the large perspex board. Position the top tier onto the tilting cake stand using some glass-headed pins.

2 Pipe some free-style rose embroidery onto the surface of both cakes using some off-white royal icing and a piping bag fitted with a No. 0 piping tube. Allow to dry and then dust the embroidery with silver-grey lustre dust. Position the top tier (on its stand) behind the base tier. Trim the cakes with rosy mauve satin ribbon.

3 Arrange the flowers into florists' white staysoft onto both the perspex plaque and the candleholder, then position these elements onto the cake. Attach pink and grey organza-type ribbons so they flow down the candleholder. I find it easier to arrange the flowers around the cake so I can follow the lines of the cake with the flowers and foliage. Wire a small single rose to sit at the base of the cake.

SILVER SEEDHEADS

4 You will need about 15 silver ball seedheads. I used paper balls to form the base for each of the seedheads as they are lighter than paste balls. Bend a large, open hook at the end of a 20- or 18-gauge wire. Apply some non-toxic hi-tack glue to the wire and thread it through the paper ball, embedding the hook into the ball. Allow to dry. Moisten the surface of the ball and cover with a fleshy layer of flowerpaste. I used a fresh brunia seedhead to texture the surface of the paste. To create further texturing, snip at the surface of the seedhead with a small pair of sharp scissors. Allow to dry, then spray silver. When dry, dust with plum, aubergine and African violet petal dusts.

'DELILAH'

'Delilah' is a wonderful pink rose with a slightly grey undertone to it. It is available all year round from florists. The flowers are a much stronger pink both in bud and at the half rose stage. I prefer the flowers when they are almost fully open since they have a better shape and the colour is a very subtle, complex pink. Unfortunately, 'Delilah', like most florists' roses, has no scent. Along with 'Leonidas', this is one of my favourite florists' roses.

PREPARATION

1 First of all you will need to squash your set of rose petal cutters into the correct shape. The 'Delilah' rose has quite rounded and broad petals (see page 156).

2 Bend a large open hook in the end of an 18-gauge wire. Form a ball of paste into a cone shape, slightly smaller than the smallest rose petal cutter in the set. Moisten the hooked wire and insert it into the base of the rose cone. Pinch some of the paste down onto the wire to secure the two together. The wire should be inserted almost to the tip of the bud. Allow to dry. If you are making rosebuds then this central cone should be slightly smaller and slimmer in shape. Colour a large amount of paste using ruby and violet food colours. It is advisable to mix a large amount, as it is always difficult to mix the exact colour again!

Materials

Pink and holly/ ivy flowerpaste (gum paste)

Ruby and violet colouring (to make the pink flowerpaste)

26- and 18-gauge white wires

Plum, white, African violet, ruby and shadow grey petal dusts

Equipment

Large set of three rose petal cutters (TT)

Very large rose petal veiner (GI)

Rose calyx cutters (OP R11b, R11c)

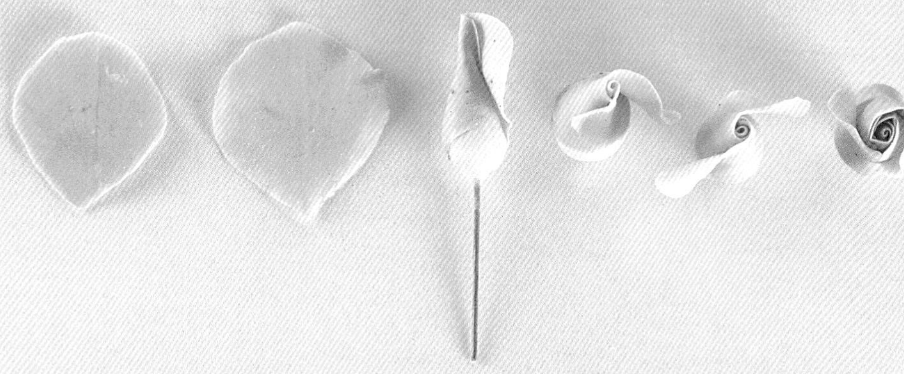

FIRST, SECOND AND THIRD LAYERS

3 Roll out some pink paste thinly, and cut out five small petals. Place the petals on a foam pad and soften the edges with a metal ball tool, working half on the paste and half on the pad. Do not try to frill the edges. Place each of the petals into the double-sided veiner and press them firmly to get a good impression.

4 Moisten the centre of one of the petals and position it against the dried cone, leaving at least 0.5cm (¼in) of the petal above the tip of the bud. Tuck the left-hand side of the petal tightly against the cone to hide the white base completely when viewed from above. Wrap the other side around to form a neat spiral, leaving the end slightly open to take the next petal.

5 Moisten the bases of the remaining four petals. Tuck the first petal under the open petal on the cone. Close the open petal over the top. Next tuck in the second petal under the first to form a tight spiral. Again, leave one petal slightly open in order to take the next petal. Repeat the process with the remaining two petals. Pinch the centre of the petals to form a central vein, and on some pinch very firmly to create a slight point. At this stage you could add a calyx to make a rosebud.

FOURTH AND FIFTH LAYERS

6 Roll out some more paste and cut out four petals using the medium cutter. Repeat the steps as for the second and third layers. Curl back the edges a little more on the last layer.

SIXTH LAYER

7 Roll out more flowerpaste and cut out three petals using the medium cutter. Soften and vein the petals as before. Position the first petal slightly under the last petal from the previous layer. Pinch the petal from the base to the edge to create a more cupped shape. Place the next petal over the join between the

previous two and then position the third slightly over the top of the second. Pinch the tips again and curl back the edges slightly. Add a calyx to make a partial half rose.

SEVENTH LAYER

8 Repeat as for the sixth layer using the largest cutter. Cup the petals a little more this time and position them over a join in the previous layer. Curl back the edges even more than before to create very pointed shapes. Add a calyx to make a half rose.

EIGHTH LAYER (WIRED PETALS)

9 Roll out a cone of pink paste, leaving a subtle thick ridge to insert a wire. Cut out a petal using the largest rose cutter again. Insert a hooked, moistened 26-gauge white wire into the base of the petal. Soften the edges and vein as before. Cup the centre of the petal and curl back the edges to form quite pointed petals. Allow to dry for a little while in an apple tray former (or you can make a former using a thick strip of kitchen paper, twisted and tied into a loop). Rest the petal until it is firm enough to handle, but not dry. Repeat to make five petals.

ASSEMBLY AND COLOURING

10 You might prefer to dust the outer five petals before you wire them onto the half rose. However, I usually assemble the flower first and then dust it as a whole flower. The backs of the petals are a much darker version of the front. Mix together plum, a little white, African violet and perhaps a touch of ruby. Dust the backs of the petals first. Then colour the centre of the rose with this mixture as well. The base of each petal should also be dusted heavily on the front. To dust the main bulk of the flower, add more white petal dust and also some shadow grey. Dust the flower all over to soften the contrast between the first dusting and the base paste colour. If the rose is still slightly wet then you should be able to re-shape the outer petals if required. Do not be tempted to steam the rose, as this will make the shadow grey very dark on the surface of the rose.

11 Add a calyx using the largest cutter for the full rose (see 'Elegance' rose, pages 105–106 for making the calyx).

TRADESCANTIA *(Tradescantia zebrina)*

Tradescantia is named after John Tradescant, gardener to King Charles I, who also introduced Virginia creeper, red maple, michaelmas daisies and *Lobelia cardinalis* to Great Britain.

Materials

Ruby coloured flowerpaste (gum paste)

28-, 26-, 22 and 20-gauge white wires

Plum, aubergine, holly/ivy and African violet petal dusts

White bridal satin petal dust

Isopropyl alcohol

Quarter or half glaze

Equipment

Plain-edged cutting wheel (PME) or various sizes of cattleya wing petal cutters

Small palette (to mix powder colours with alcohol)

Small paintbrush

Nile green floristry tape

1 Roll out some pale ruby flowerpaste, leaving a thick ridge at the centre. Cut out a basic leaf shape with one of the cattleya orchid cutters, or freestyle using the plain-edged cutting wheel, or failing that a scalpel. Insert a moistened 28- or 26-gauge white wire (depending upon the size of the leaf) into the thick ridge to about half the length of the leaf.

2 Soften the edges with either a metal ball tool or the rounded end of a large celstick. The edges should be plain and not frilled. Vein the surface of the leaf with the fine end of the dresden tool. The leaves are quite flat with their veining and it is painted work that creates the interest with this foliage. Pinch the leaf at the base and again at the tip and allow to dry (not completely) with a slight curve, mainly at the tip.

DUSTING AND ASSEMBLY

3 It is best to use a real plant or close-up photograph as reference when painting detailed leaves. Dust the backs and fronts heavily with African violet and plum petal dusts. Overdust the edges and centres with aubergine petal dust. Holly/ivy can be added to the central section of the leaf.

4 Paint in the detailed marking using a small paintbrush and some white bridal satin dust mixed with a touch of holly/ivy and isopropyl alcohol. Only paint two or three silvery lines onto each leaf. Create extra depth by diluting aubergine dust and adding some detailed marking to the edge and centre of the leaf.

5 The leaves do not have a gloss as such but you might prefer to glaze them using a quarter or even a half glaze, though the leaves will lose some of their silvery sheen when dipped into glaze.

6 Tape the leaves in a trailing manner onto 22-gauge wire. Gradually add further 20-gauge wires to the stem for support, using half-width tape. Dust the stems with holly/ivy and a touch of plum at the junction of each leaf. Bend the stem to give it a trailing formation.

Arum Lily

(*Zantedeschia aethiopica*)

Zantedeschia lilies have become a favourite of florists and cake decorators alike. They are simple to make and form a graceful addition to a cake, whether used as the main subject or with other flowers. Colour varies from white, yellow, pink, orange, green, red and burgundy to almost black.

Materials

Ruby coloured flowerpaste (gum paste)

18-gauge wire

Aubergine, plum, African violet and holly/ivy petal dusts

Equipment

Small nutmeg grater

Sharp scalpel or plain-edged cutting wheel (PME)

Extra large amaryllis veiner (GI)

Arum lily template (see page 156)

Nile green floristry tape

SPADIX

1 Roll a medium-sized ball of well-kneaded ruby flowerpaste and then insert an 18-gauge wire. Work the paste firmly between your fingers and thumb to cover a length of about 4.5cm ($1\frac{3}{4}$in) of the wire. Smooth the shape between your palms and then remove the excess paste. Texture the surface of the spadix with a nutmeg grater. Attach a ball of paste at the base of the spadix, which will act as a padding to the base of the flower later on. Dust the spadix heavily with a mixture of aubergine, plum and African violet petal dusts. Allow to dry.

SPATHE

2 Roll out some more ruby-coloured flowerpaste, though not too fine. Place the spathe template (see page 156) on top of the paste and cut around the shape using a sharp scalpel or the plain-edged cutting wheel. Place the shape onto the amaryllis veiner, positioning with the point of a celstick or metal ball tool. Using the fine end of a dresden tool, add a few extra central veins.

3 Moisten the base of the spathe with fresh egg white (do not attempt to try this with edible glue or gum arabic solution). Then place the spadix on either the left- or the right-hand side, both of which are an option to the real flower. Gently roll the two together. Curl back the edges, particularly the long edge that overlaps. Pinch and work the tip into a very fine point and then leave them hanging upside down, until the paste is firm enough to be re-shaped a little.

4 Thicken the main stem with more 18-gauge wire, a little shredded kitchen paper and some full-width nile green floristry tape.

COLOURING

5 The flowers pictured have been dusted heavily with aubergine, plum and African violet petal dusts. The base and the tips were dusted with holly/ivy petal dust. Once the flower has dried, steam it to set the colour and to lend it a slight sheen.

The inspiration for this cake came when I saw a group of dog's-tooth violets growing in a friend's garden. I thought they were lovely, fragile little flowers that would look wonderful presented alongside an open rose. The unusual dappled leaves add depth and interest to this cake. *–Tony*

Summer Solstice

Cake and Decoration

25cm (10in) scalloped oval cake
Apricot glaze
850g (1¾lb) white almond paste (marzipan)
Clear alcohol (kirsch or Cointreau)
1.25kg (2¾lb) champagne sugarpaste (cold rolled fondant)
3mm tangerine ribbon
Ivory feathered-edge 9mm (⅓in) ribbon
Royal icing
Melon paste colour
Flowerpaste (gum paste)
Cornflour (cornstarch)
White vegetable fat
Lemon, white and tangerine petal dusts
Nile green floristry tape

Flowers

1 full 'Chicago' rose
3 half 'Chicago' roses
3 'Chicago' rosebuds
3 sprays of rose leaves
5 dog's-tooth violets
3 dog's-tooth violet leaves
7 sprays of ruscus

Equipment

32cm (13in) oval cake drum
Non-toxic glue stick
No. 1 piping tube
Lace cutter of choice (DL)
Posy pick
Long-nosed pliers

1 Bake a cake in a medium scalloped oval cake tin. Prepare the cake by using the scallop on the side of the tin as the template. Use a very sharp knife to cut around the shape. Brush with apricot glaze and cover with almond paste. Allow to dry. Moisten the almond paste with clear alcohol and cover with sugarpaste, covering the cake drum at the same time. Use smoothers to achieve a good finish to the sugarpaste. Then take a handful of sugarpaste, polish it and polish the whole of the cake, especially the edges. Work quickly or the sugarpaste will stick.

2 Place the cake on the board and attach tangerine ribbon around the base with a little royal icing. Position the join in the ribbon in the front curve of the cake, which will be hidden by the spray. Trim the board with the ivory ribbon and attach using a non-toxic glue stick. Colour a little royal icing with melon paste colour and then pipe a snail's trail around the cake base.

LACE

3 Calculate how many lace pieces you need. Colour some flowerpaste with the melon colour to achieve a similar tone to the sugarpaste covering the cake. Stiffen the flowerpaste with additional cornflour. Cut out thin pieces of lace and remove from the cutter by pressing into a dab of white vegetable fat. Place the lace pieces on a flat surface, preferably porous, to dry. Dust the tips with lemon dust lightened with white petal dust. Overdust lightly with the tangerine dust. Attach the lace pieces to the cake with royal icing.

ASSEMBLY

4 Tape the half roses and dog's-tooth violets around the open rose. Add the small rosebuds in between. Now tape in the dog's-tooth violet leaves, then the ruscus and lastly the rose leaves. Insert the stem of the spray into the posy pick and, using the long-nosed pliers, insert the pick into the cake. Take care not to knock off the lace pieces.

'CHICAGO'

The Chicago rose is a hybrid Tea Rose raised by Johnston in America and introduced into Great Britain in 1962. The plant has an upright, bushy growth with pleasantly scented, warm-tinted flowers that open out to reveal lightly frilled petals.

Materials

Small white hammer-head stamens

30-, 28-, 26- and 18-gauge wires

Pale melon and pale green flowerpaste (gum paste)

Non-toxic hi-tack glue

White, primrose, lemon, Cornish cream, tangerine, plum, holly/ivy, moss green, rosé and white bridal satin petal dusts

Equipment

Tweezers

Nile green floristry tape

Dimpled foam

Rose templates (see page 150)

Very large rose petal veiner (GI)

Calyx cutter (OP R11b)

Curved scissors

1 To make the centre for your open rose, glue about 25 stamens, with their filaments folded in two, to the top of a one-third length 18-gauge wire. The outer stamens are longer than those in the centre and should be made to curve inwards with a pair of tweezers. Tape over the base of the stamens with half-width nile green floristry tape. Dust the filaments of the stamens with rosé, then the anthers with lemon dust.

2 Roll out pale melon flowerpaste in a sausage to leave a thickened edge. Cut out three stamenoids (small narrow petals) using the petal template on page 150. Moisten the end of a quarter-length 30-gauge wire and insert into the thickened paste at the base. Place on a foam pad and soften the edges. Vein with the petal veiner and curve using the rounded edge of a celpin.

3 Using the next sized template, continue cutting out petals, with the point over the thickened paste. You will need five petals for each layer. Moisten the end of a 30-gauge quarter-length wire and insert into the thickened paste. Soften the edges, then vein and cup each petal as before. Place on dimpled foam to dry.

4 Cut out another three petals from the rolled-out paste using the third size template. Moisten the end of quarter-length 28-gauge wire and repeat the process as described above. Continue until all eight layers have been made.

COLOURING

5 Starting with the inner petals, dust with lemon and tangerine dusts. Repeat

this colouring, but lighten it slightly with white petal dust. Dust the third layer with Cornish cream and then overdust with pale lemon at the base of the petals. Then, delicately touch the tips with some pale plum dust.

6 Repeat this process – lightening the colour very slightly for each layer. Petals in the last layer have only a light dusting of Cornish cream and lemon but a slightly increased dusting of the pale plum dust.

ASSEMBLY

7 Starting with the stamenoids and gradually increasing the size, tape the petals onto the 18-gauge wire, immediately behind the stamens, using half-width floristry tape. Tug down on the loose ends to ensure the wires are not showing. Continue until all the petals are taped in place. Each layer should go across the join of the previous layer. Arrange the petals attractively so that the central petals curve inwards. To create a half rose, add the calyx after the fourth layer.

CALYX

8 Roll out pale green paste into a cone, then pinch out the thick end to form a circle. Place on a non-stick board and use a celpin to fine out the paste. Place the cutter over the pedicel and cut out the calyx. Elongate each sepal slightly with the celpin. Place the calyx on a foam pad and soften the edges with the back of the celpin. Hollow the centre of the sepals once again using the same tool. Cut fine hairs at the edge of the

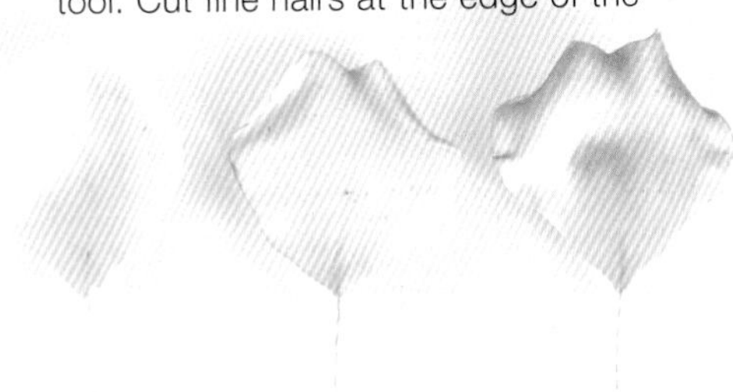

sepals using the curved scissors. Dust the inside of the calyx with white bridal satin dust and the outside with moss green petal dust, adding a slash of holly/ivy up the centre. Leave the edges pale.

9 Moisten the centre and attach the calyx to the back of the petals. Curve the sepals back. Leave to dry. Steam the flower to set the dust.

QUICK ROSEBUDS

10 Make small, rounded, chubby cones. Moisten the end of a one-third length hooked 18-gauge wire and insert into the cone. Use a craft knife to cut angled grooves into the cone. Gently lift the edges to make it look as though the petals are opening. Dust these cones with lemon petal dust, lightening it towards the tip of the cone. Dust a little tangerine into the grooves and overdust with the rosé petal dust.

11 Use green paste to form the calyx as described above, sticking the sepals to the side of the bud, over the cut grooves. Curl back one or two of the sepals to give a sense of movement to the bud.

LARGER ROSEBUDS

12 These rosebuds are made in the same manner as for the 'Pink Favourite' rose (see pages 64–5).

ROSE LEAVES

13 The rose leaves used in the arrangement for this cake are created using the same method as the leaves for the 'Elegance' rose (see pages 104–6).

Dog's-Tooth Violet (*Erythronium*)

These are pretty, spring-flowering bulbous plants. They were first introduced from Europe in the late 16th century. Their common name comes from the shape of the bulb. They look nothing like violets, but the Elizabethans called almost half the plants they grew violets of some sort. Their elegant petals are strongly reflexed but the leaves, too, are often marked with liver-coloured or darker green blotches on a paler background, which gives them the appearance, recently described by Alan, of battle camouflage!

Materials

28-, 24- and 22-gauge white wires
Long, slender stamens
Lemon, primrose, vine green, aubergine, brown and moss petal dusts
Pale melon and pale to mid-green flowerpaste (gum paste)
Ruby red paste colour
Isopropyl alcohol
Half glaze

Equipment

White and nile green floristry tape
Dog's-tooth violet petal template (see page 157)
Plain-edged cutting wheel (PME)
Silicone Plastique homemade dog's-tooth violet petal and leaf veiners (see page 34)
No. 2 paintbrush
Long-nosed pliers
Dog's-tooth violet leaf template (see page 157)

PISTIL AND STAMENS

1 To form the pistil, take a one-third length of 22-gauge wire. Cut white floristry tape in half and then use sharp scissors to cut the half-width piece of white tape into three sections, each about 1.25cm (½in) long. Leave the split tape loose above the wire, and bind the rest of the tape down the length of the wire.

2 Rub your fingers firmly up and down a whole piece of tape to make your fingers tacky. Now twist each of the

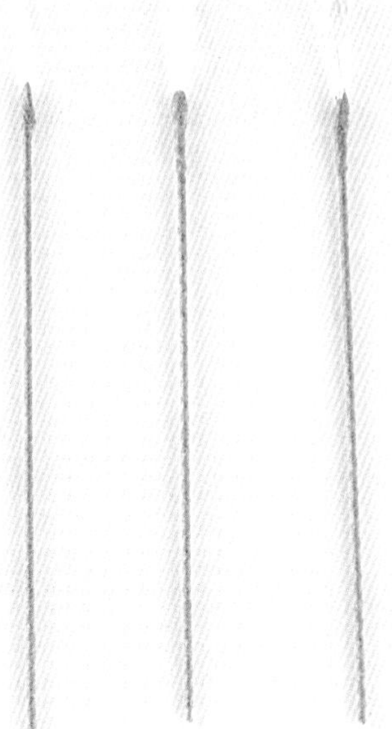

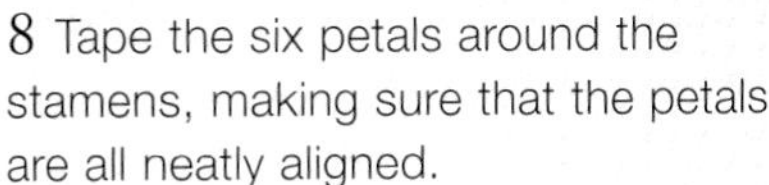

pieces of split tape to form neat, tight strands. Cut these off quite short.

3 Tape the stamens around the pistil, leaving the tip of the pistil above the stamens. Dust the stamens and pistil with pale lemon dust.

PETALS

4 Roll the melon paste into a sausage, leaving one edge thicker. Place the petal template from page 157 over the paste and use the cutting wheel to cut out six petals.

5 Moisten the end of a quarter-length 28-gauge wire and insert it into the thickened end of the paste.

6 Place the petals on a foam pad and soften the edges with the rounded end of a celpin. Vein the petals with your homemade dog's-tooth violet veiner. Place on dimpled foam to dry.

7 Dust the base of the petals with primrose and vine green petal dust. Ensure the dusting on the back of the petals is paler than in the centre of the flower. Dust the tips of the petals with vine green dust.

8 Tape the six petals around the stamens, making sure that the petals are all neatly aligned.

9 Mix some ruby colour with a little isopropyl alcohol and use this to paint a chevron of red on the inside of each petal, as illustrated above.

10 Tape the stem of the flowers to thicken them slightly.

11 Use long-nosed pliers to hold the wire immediately behind the petals, then curve the neck of the flower into a graceful curve.

12 The buds of the dog's-tooth violet are seldom seen, but are long and slender and shaped rather like lily buds. You can mark them with a wire cage, six wires divided into three sets of two.

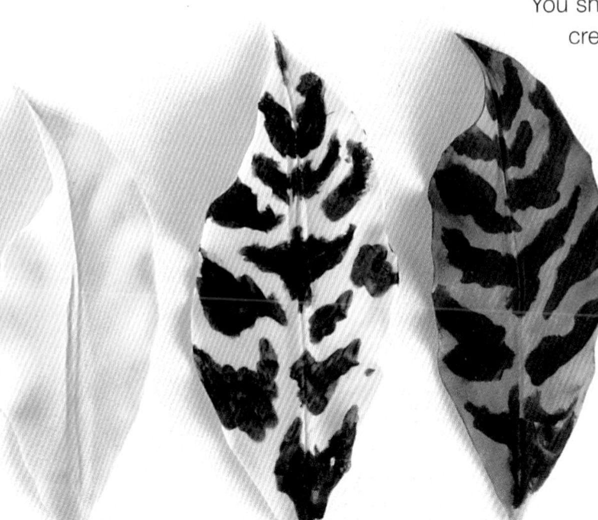

LEAVES

13 Roll out a sausage of pale to mid-green paste, roll the sides out thinly with the celpin. Insert a moistened, one-third length 24-gauge wire into the thickened paste. Place on a board and cut around the template using the cutting wheel.

14 Place the leaf on the foam pad, soften the edges and vein the leaf using the double-sided dog's-tooth violet veiner. Accentuate the central veins using the veiner tool and a dresden tool. Place on dimpled foam to dry.

15 Mix the aubergine and a little bit of the brown petal dust with clear alcohol and paint 'camouflage' marks over the surface of the leaf.

16 When this painted area is dry, overdust with moss green petal dust. You should also use a little brown to create shading.

17 Tape the leaf stems with the white floristry tape and dust the stems along one edge with the dark brown/green petal dust. The other side of the stems is much paler so ensure you give it a lighter dusting.

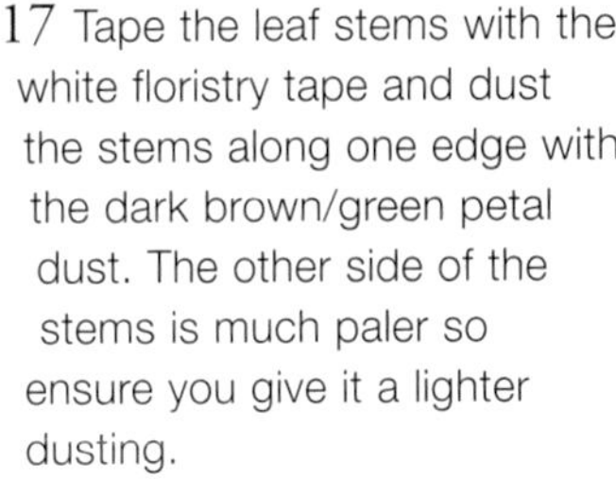

18 Steam the flowers and leaves to set the dust. Glaze the leaves with half glaze.

Ruscus

The small nodules of the ruscus that appear to be leaves are, in fact, a type of modified and flattened stem called cladodes. These, particularly those of the large-leaf variety, produce tiny flowers that are followed by small red fruit.

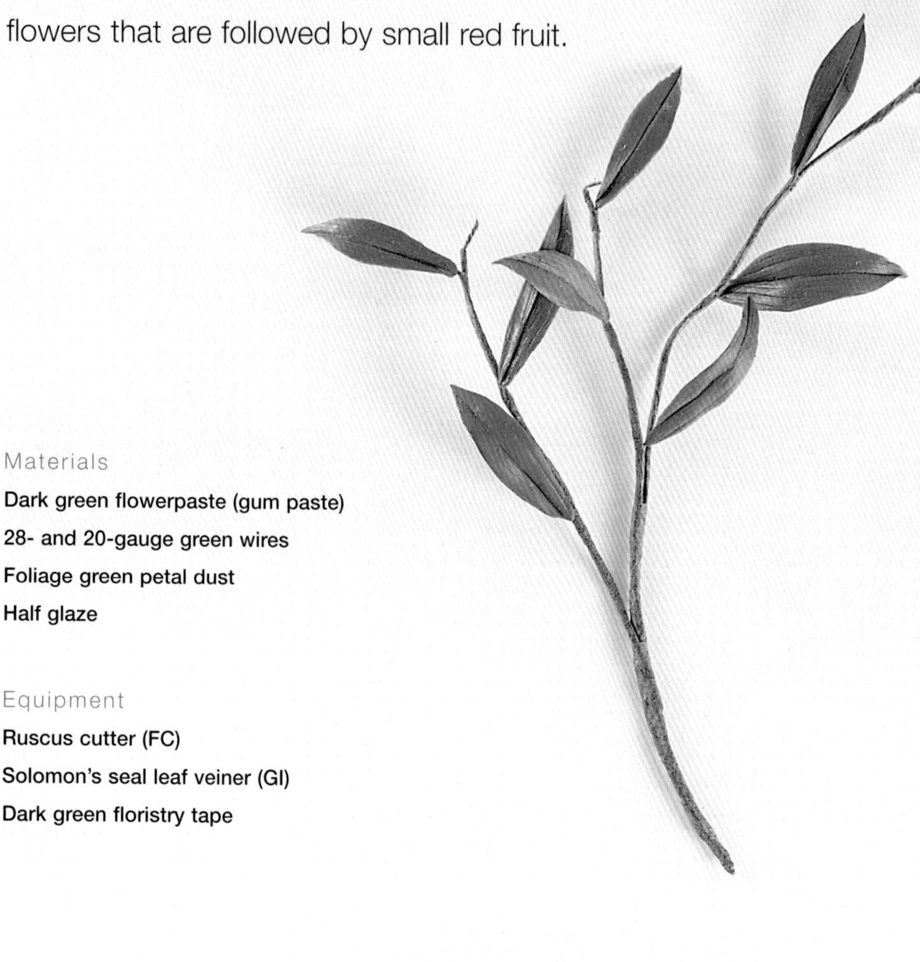

Materials

Dark green flowerpaste (gum paste)
28- and 20-gauge green wires
Foliage green petal dust
Half glaze

Equipment

Ruscus cutter (FC)
Solomon's seal leaf veiner (GI)
Dark green floristry tape

1 Roll out a quantity of dark green flowerpaste, leaving a thicker central ridge, and then cut out the cladode with the ruscus cutter.

2 Moisten a quarter-length 28-gauge wire with egg white and insert it into the thick ridge. The wire should go quite a way up the length of the cladode.

3 Next vein the cladode using the Solomon's seal veiner. Pinch the cladode at both the base and tip. Repeat this process to make the required number of cladodes.

COLOURING AND ASSEMBLY

4 Heavily dust the cladode with the foliage green petal dust. Once dry, dip into the half glaze.

5 Tape the cladodes together into groups of two and three. Then tape these groups in turn onto a 20-gauge green wire, starting with one set of cladodes and then spiralling the others down the stem.

6 Dust the stems of the ruscus using the foliage green petal dust.

Corsages

Roses are the most popular of bridal flowers and are often used in button holes and corsages. It is important not to make a corsage too heavy, as in theory these are intended to be worn. Here are three examples of rose corsages, each complemented by different plant material. Most of the sprays featured in this book can be adapted to create a corsage. The elements of one design can be mixed with those of another.

PINK ROSE CORSAGE (top left)
This corsage uses only a half rose as its focal point. A single white blossom, purple appleberries and jasmine leaves have been used to complement the rose. The corsage has been completed with some fine green ribbon loops.

PLUM ROSE CORSAGE (bottom left)
The variegated colouring of tradescantia leaves used with this single, full rose beautifully picks up the mauvey-blue of the flower. Mahonia berries continue the colour theme and add some extra detail to the corsage.

RED ROSE CORSAGE (below)
This rather unusual modern corsage features an orange-red rose as its focal flower, complemented by a prominent set of rose leaves, a pink and red gymea lily, and single trailing stems of *Celastrus* and *Crocosmia* berries.

This cake is named after my gem of a granddaughter, Pero, whose enquiring little fingers forced me to make last minute changes to the surface of the cake. I feel that these changes have improved it! The arrangement of the top tier was to create the illusion that it was 'floating' on the main rose spray. –*Tombi*

Pero's Pearl Cake

Cake and Decoration

30cm (12in), 25cm (10in) and 18cm (7in) round cakes covered in almond paste (marzipan) and sugarpaste (cold rolled fondant)

60g (2oz) flowerpaste (gum paste) mixed with 60g (2oz) white sugarpaste

Clear alcohol (kirsch or Cointreau)

Cherry red ribbon to trim board

Flowers

3 full white 'Elegance' roses (see pages 104–6)

5 half 'Elegance' roses

10 'Elegance' rosebuds

12 sets of rose leaves

9 blood lilies (see pages 114–15)

Equipment

Rosebud and opposing rose leaf leather punches

White nylon bristled no. 2 paintbrush

Non-toxic glue stick

Nile green floristry tape

Flower pick

1 small celnest with 8 holes burnt into front and sides with heated skewer (C)

2 bags clear glass floristry beads

1 First cover the three cakes with a layers of almond paste and sugarpaste. Then knead the equal amounts of flowerpaste and sugarpaste together. Leave overnight. Roll out the mixed paste very thinly and cut out plenty of roses and leaves with the leather punches. Moisten these shapes with clear alcohol, using the paintbrush, and stick them in place as shown. Finish with a decorative border of leaves around the base. The joins between the cakes and boards of the middle and bottom tiers are finished with a similar border. Attach the red ribbon to the board with the glue stick.

2 To make the top tier spray, tape together one rose, two sets of leaves, two buds and three blood lilies. Push the end of the spray into a food grade flower pick and push the flower pick into the top tier, leaving the rim visible.

3 Tape together another spray to place alongside the cake, consisting of one rose, one rosebud, three sets of leaves and three blood lilies. Tape up the remaining flowers into attractive small sprays.

4 Centre the celnest on the middle tier and then fill it three-quarters full with glass floristry beads. This will prevent the celnest tipping over as you insert the sprays. Arrange the flowers attractively in the celnest. Very carefully test whether the flowers are the right height to take the top tier. If you are satisfied the flower sprays are in the correct position, fill the celnest with the remaining glass beads.

5 The final assembly of the cake should only be done in situ. Gently place the top tier in position, then carefully arrange the flowers just below the top tier to leave small spaces allowing you to see through the arrangement. Position the central rose to hide the celnest and glass beads. Place the remaining spray at the base of the cake.

I have wanted to try out a quilted design, so I found a very simple rose design, which I thought would be ideal. The design can be worked onto a cake that has been coated as usual, but in my mind's eye I visualized the cake as a quilted box and decided to create what I visualized. —*Tombi*

Quilted Box Cake

Cake and Decoration

Heart shaped cake, 20cm (8in) from dip to tip

20cm (8in) heart-shaped board

1.75kg (3¾lb) champagne sugarpaste (cold rolled fondant)

Apricot purée

1.25kg (2¾lb) white almond paste (marzipan)

Clear alcohol (kirsch or Cointreau)

250g (8oz) flowerpaste (gum paste)

Vine green, holly/ivy green and lemon yellow petal dusts

Alabaster, double cream and myrtle bridal satin dusts

Flower

'Pascali' rose with vine leaves

Equipment

Pair of dividers

Watermarked silk rolling pin (HP)

Pizza wheel

Dupion silk rolling pin (HP)

Fan-shaped leather punch

Dressmakers' stitching wheel

Rose design template (see page 155)

Scriber

PREPARATION

1 Invert the cake so that the base is uppermost and fill in any dents with almond paste. Roll sausages of sugarpaste and insert them under the edge of the cake where it does not meet the board, cutting off the excess with a flat-bladed knife. Ensure the cake is level. Smooth over with a smoother. Apply warmed apricot purée to the surface of the cake with a pastry brush.

2 Roll out the almond paste, lift it over the cake and smooth it down, making sure you do not trap any air. Stroke with smoothers and then polish the surface of the cake with your hands.

3 Decide on how far down the side of your cake the lid of your box will go. Use a pair of dividers to mark a straight line around the side of the cake.

FORMING THE BOX

4 Make a large roll of champagne sugarpaste and fasten this to the side of the cake with clear alcohol, making sure the roll of paste is even all around the cake.

5 Once again, draw a straight line on the roll of sugarpaste where the edge of the box is to be positioned. Then, using a pair of smoothers, work the paste to form a neatly angled wedge shape all around the cake. There should be no dips or bumps as this will destroy the box-like look. If there are any hollows, fill them with extra sugarpaste. Allow to dry completely.

6 Use a sharp, smooth-bladed knife to ensure angles are sharp and that the surfaces are flat. Fill in any dents with extra sugarpaste. Ensure the edge is sharp and level with the table.

7 Mix 250g (8oz) flowerpaste with an equal amount of the champagne sugarpaste. Roll out a strip of this mixed paste wide enough to extend from the board to the line you have drawn around the cake, forming the join in the box, and long enough to extend around the cake. This strip should not be rolled too thinly as you still need to texture it. Roll it out again using the watermarked silk rolling pin.

8 Cut out the strip using a straight edge and pizza wheel. Moisten the area where the strip will be attached. Lightly dust the strip with a little cornflour (cornstarch) and roll the strip up like a bandage. Begin to attach the roll to the cake, starting at the tip. Concentrate on getting the line straight.

9 Due to the angle between the wedge and the board, you will need to pleat the paste where it meets the board. Use a very sharp pair of scissors to cut away the excess paste. This should not spoil the design too much. The pleated

edge at the bottom of the cake will be less visible because of the overhang.

10 Roll out another strip of mixed paste broad enough to extend from the sharp edge to the upper edge. Ensure it is not too thin as it will need to be textured. It should only be a little longer than the measurement from the dip at the back to the point. Texture the strip, this time using the dupion silk rolling pin.

11 Cut the strip neatly once again with a straight edge and a pizza wheel. Moisten the area where the strip will be attached. Starting this time at the point, carefully attach the strip to the cake, making sure that you get a very neat join where you form the lid of the box. Ease the paste around the curve. If this is done very gently you will not need to pleat the paste. Cut the paste off neatly in the dip. Repeat for the other side. Use the leather punch to neaten the joins while the paste is still soft.

12 Roll out a piece of paste large enough to cover the top of the cake. Texture with the watermarked rolling pin. Use the cake tin to make a template, cut the piece of paste out, moisten the top surface of the cake and attach it to the cake. Cut off any pieces that may overlap the edging strip. Gently tuck in any stray edges. Neaten the edge of the strip with the leather punch. Mark a few 'patches' onto the surface with your stitching wheel. Allow to set.

ROSE DESIGN

13 Enlarge the template to the required size. Make a tracing of the design, tracing the outer edge just fractionally inside the design with your scriber, pricking through the tracing onto the textured surface. This will ensure when you transfer the design to the cake none of the scribed markings will be showing once you have added the 'fabric'.

14 Cut out separate templates for the various pieces required. Start with the pieces that are recessed. To create a good patchwork look, do not have all the textures running in the same direction.

15 Pad the raised areas with plain sugarpaste. Roll out the textured pieces of paste and cut them out using your template. Always allow extra paste where the 'fabric' is lifted over rolls or tucked under to create a lifted edge. Once all the pieces are in place, use the stitching wheel to mark veins onto the petals.

16 Dust the sepals and stem with a little vine and holly/ivy dust. Use lemon yellow to define the heart of the rose and where the two front petals are joined. Now dust over the whole of the rose and the top surface of the cake with double cream bridal satin. Use alabaster bridal satin to create highlights on the rose. Use myrtle bridal satin on the stem and sepals.

17 Finally, position the single 'Pascali' rose backed by vine leaves alongside the cake.

‘Pascali’

‘Pascali’ is a hybrid Tea Rose, white with hints of yellow and cream and dark green leaves. I have vine leaves which are a softer green when young. I felt the contrast against a creamy white cake would be too severe. The buds reflex their petal tips very prettily.

Materials

Very pale melon and pale green flowerpaste (gum paste)

28, 26 and 18-gauge wires

Lemon, vine green and holly/ivy green petal dusts

Bridal satin dust

Half glaze

Equipment

Very large rose petal veiner (GI)

Rose petal cutters (TT549, 550, 551)

Smooth porcelain tool (HP)

Large and medium black plastic rose leaf cutters (J)

Large green plastic rose petal cutter (J)

Rose calyx cutter (OP R11A)

Large briar rose leaf veiner (GI)

Large green plastic rose leaf cutter (J)

Nile green floristry tape

To create the structure of the rose head for the ‘Pascali’ rose, follow steps 1–7 for the ‘Elegance’ rose on pages 104–5, then proceed as follows:

COLOURING AND ASSEMBLING THE ROSE

1 When the petals are almost dry, add a little lemon dust at the base of each wired petal, then a touch of vine green. It is amazing how such an apparently insignificant touch of colour will bring the rose to life. Using a very fine brush, add some yellow down the throat of the rose.

2 Tape the wired petals in place with half-width floristry tape. I have developed the habit of taping three petals in place and then bringing the next two petals inside those already taped in place. It seems to improve the look of the rose.

3 Add the largest petals. If one of the slightly smaller wired petals does not look right when you wire them together, remove it and wire it in behind the large petals. This rose often has some rather untidy smaller petals behind the largest.

4 Make sure all the petals are in the right place before you add the calyx.

CALYX

5 Roll a piece of pale green paste into a ball. Then roll it again into the shape of a cone and pinch out the broad end of the cone into a circle.

6 Place the circle on the board and roll out the paste with a medium celstick. Place the cutter over the pedicel and cut out the shape. Elongate each of the sepals by rolling them with the celstick.

7 Place the sepals one at a time on a foam pad and stroke down the centre of the sepal with a dresden tool. Repeat this using the veining end.

8 Make an indentation in the centre of the calyx with the back of a celstick.

9 Dust the inside of the calyx with the white bridal satin dust. When the calyx is dry, steam the rose to set the dust.

10 Cut fine hairs along the edges of the sepals with a sharp pair of scissors.

11 Moisten the centre of the calyx with egg white and stick it behind the petals, positioning the sepals at the junction of the petals.

12 Dust the centre of the back of the calyx with holly/ivy petal dust, leaving the edges pale.

ASSEMBLY

13 To assemble the single rose spray, tape three vine leaves behind the ‘Pascali’ rose with nile green floristry tape. Instructions for making the vine leaves can be found on page 113.

'ELEGANCE'

This is a good, standard modern rose shape which, with a little working of the wired petal shapes and different colouring, can be transformed into many specific roses. The wired petals enable the rose to be wired in tightly against other flowers and leaves as the movement allowed by the wired petals gives the rose some flexibility.

Materials

Very pale melon and mid-green flowerpaste (gum paste)

26- and 18-gauge white wires

Lemon, vine green, rosé, holly/ivy, and forest (dark) green petal dusts

White bridal satin dust

Cornflour (cornstarch)

Quarter glaze

Equipment

Very large rose petal veiner (GI)

Rose petal cutters (TT549, 550, 551)

Smooth porcelain tool (HP)

Large and medium black plastic rose leaf cutters (J)

Large green plastic rose petal cutter (J)

Rose calyx cutter (TT245 or OP R11)

Large green plastic rose leaf cutter (J)

Large briar rose leaf veiner (GI)

Nile green floristry tape

Fleximat

Dimpled foam

CONE

1 Take a piece of the pale melon paste and roll it into a smooth ball, then into a long, pointed cone with a broad base. Moisten a half-length 18-gauge hooked wire and insert it into the base of the cone. The cone should be no longer than the smallest petal you are using to make the rose. For buds, it should be at least 0.5cm (¼in) smaller than the small cutter size. The cones must be very dry before attempting to add any petals.

PETALS

2 Roll out some pale melon paste – not too fine, or there will be no movement in your petals. Take a petal, place it on a foam pad and soften the edge with a metal ball tool. Dust the petal veiner with cornflour and vein the petal. Moisten the petal and place the cone on the petal. If you are making a bud, make sure the base of the cone is covered by the petal, but if you are making a full or half rose, concentrate only on the top edge of the petal. Roll the petal around the cone, creating a very tight spiral at the tip. (You must not be able to see the cone at all.) Prepare all the rose cones like this. If you are creating a bud, you can roll the edge back very slightly.

3 Cut out three petals, using the smallest of the four petal shapes; leave two petals under a fleximat while you work on the other. Soften the edge and vein the petal. Repeat this for the other petals. Moisten down the left-hand side of the petals, about three-quarters of the length of the petal. Place the rose cone onto the first petal and stick the petal in place ensuring that it is higher than that of the first layer. Add the other two petals, tucking them one inside the other. Loosely spiral them around the cone. Moisten the loose edge of both petals and, with a slight twist, pull down and fasten the petals onto the cone.

Using the smooth porcelain tool, roll back the edges of the petals slightly to make a rose. To make a bud, roll back one more strongly than the other. You can make about five centres at a time, before the sugar becomes hard.

4 Repeat step 3. Tuck the petals under those of the second layer. Add another three petals using the second sized cutter, still keeping the petals tight. If you are creating a bud, at this stage you can loosen the petals slightly, concentrating on getting a neat base to the flower and giving graceful curls to the edges of the petals.

5 To create the half rose, increase the size of the petal cutter again and repeat as before. Now cup the petals using metal ball tool or by pressing hard into the petal with your thumb. If you have a base in which the points of the petal are visible, you can move up to the largest cutter, but I prefer to reserve this for my wired petals. With this layer, tuck only the first petal below one from the previous layer – the others are spiralled around the cone. At this stage, you can add a calyx to form your half rose.

WIRED PETALS

6 Roll the paste, so that it is a little thicker at the pointed base of the petals. Cut 26-gauge wires into quarters and hook one end of each length. Cut out a petal using the largest cutter (the green plastic cutter), placing the pointed end of the cutter over the thickened paste. Moisten a piece of wire and insert the hooked end into the thickened piece of paste. Repeat the moulding of each petal, cupping each one and creating the natural-looking curves and rolls that typify the rose you are copying.

7 Soften the edges of the outer petals by working the edges with a frilling tool over the forefinger of your left hand. Many roses have their petals rolled back so strongly that it gives an almost triangular look to the petal as you look at it from the top of the rose. Make ten wired petals for each rose.

COLOURING AND ASSEMBLY

8 Start by dusting a little pale lemon onto the base of each petal (at the wire) on both the back and front and down the throat of the rose. Be careful not to get the yellow onto the edges of the petal. This rose should not look too yellow, so lightly dust the colour onto the petal to give a glow only. Add a touch of vine green at the wire.

9 Tape the petals onto the centre, making sure that you are taping tightly against it. Pull down on the wires to bed the petals into place. You will achieve a better look by wiring the first three petals in place, then pulling the other two petals inside them. Then add the slightly larger petals. Each rose will use eight to twelve petals; you can judge when a rose looks complete. Once all the petals are wired, place tape over the full length of the wire using full-width tape, steeply angled to give a smooth stem to your rose. This can be improved by polishing the tape with the back of a knife.

10 Now add the colour to the centre of the rose. Load the flat, soft-bristled brush with the rosé and tap it off against a piece of kitchen paper to get rid of any loose or excess dust. Dab the rosé straight into the centre of the rose twice, then very gently brush sideways across the centre to achieve an even colouring.

CALYX

11 Roll green paste into a ball, then into a cone and pinch out flat leaving a narrow pedicel. Roll out the paste with a medium celstick. Put the calyx cutter over the pedicel and cut out the shape. Roll each sepal slightly longer than the pedicel, and soften the edges on a foam pad. Cut fine hairs on the edges of the sepals with fine scissors. Cup each sepal and the centre of the calyx.

12 Dust the inside of the calyx with white bridal satin dust, then run down

the centre of each sepal with a dresden tool. Dust the outside of the sepal with holly/ivy green, being careful to leave the edges of the sepals pale. With the side of a flat dusting brush, dust a slash of dark green dust down the centre. Moisten the centre of the calyx and stick in place, ensuring the sepals cover the joins between the petals. Use a small celstick or cocktail stick (toothpick) to mark the beginning of the rose hip. If the calyx is being attached to a bud, stick several sepals against the petals. These are usually the sepals without cuts. Arrange the other sepals attractively.

LEAVES

13 Choosing the finest groove possible, roll out the mid-green paste along the groove, place the moistened wire along the groove and roll it with the rolling pin. Fold back the rolled paste from beyond the groove until it touches the edge of the board. Roll out again, sandwiching the wire between two layers of paste. Place the cutter over the groove and cut out the leaf. Soften the edge of the leaf with a ball tool on a foam pad. Dust the veiner with a little cornflour, then vein the leaf. Tweak with the fingers to give some interesting shapes. Leave to dry on dimpled foam.

14 Dust the leaves before they are dry to ensure a good depth of colour. Layer the colour for best results. Ensure that the underside of the leaf is paler than the upper surface. Use rosé on the edge of the leaves to provide more interest, then glaze with a quarter glaze. You will need one large, two medium and two smaller leaves for each group. Tape them together with half-width tape, taping a short length of wire on each leaflet. Tape these onto the main stems with the buds and flowers.

A Basket of Roses

I brought back this basket (right) from South Africa many years ago and sprayed it a mossy green, which made it very dark. An overspray of metallic pearl gave the look I wanted. –*Tombi*

SPRAY 1

1 full 'Elegance' rose

2 half 'Elegance' roses

7 'Elegance' rosebuds: 11 layers, 22 layers and 23 layers

7 sets of dark green compound rose leaves

4.5cm (1¾in) width aqua silk chiffon ribbon bow

SPRAY 2

3 full 'Elegance' roses

2 half 'Elegance' roses

5 'Elegance' rosebuds: 33 layers

6 sets dark green compound rose leaves

4.5cm (1¾in) width aqua silk chiffon ribbon

ASSEMBLY

1 Wire the roses into the sprays and tie a bow with the aqua silk chiffon ribbon.

2 As these roses are not arranged on a food product they could be made using the same method as above, but with cold porcelain paste instead.

3 You can put whatever you like into the basket. For wedding celebrations why not fill the basket with dried rose petals for confetti or wrapped slices of wedding cake. As an Easter treat for a child (or young-at-heart adult!) you could fill it with chocolates or it could be used to gather easter eggs hidden by the Easter Bunny!

This hand-tied bouquet is created from 'Breath of Life' roses, which vary from deep to light orange depending upon how far they have opened. They are combined with blood lilies which add an exotic touch. The whole arrangement is finished off by vine leaves surrounding the roses. *–Tombi*

Flamenco Hand-Tied Bouquet

Flowers

5 full 'Breath of Life' roses
5 half 'Breath of Life' roses
5 'Breath of Life' rosebuds
12 stems of vine leaves
15 blood lilies

Materials and Equipment

Nile green floristry tape
Floristry binding wire
Vase
Glass floristry beads
2 sheets of orange tissue paper
Elasticized decorative cord
Orange organza ribbon

PREPARATION

1 Make sure that all the stems are long enough, so that they may be trimmed when the bouquet is complete. If necessary, extend the length of the wires by taping alongside those forming the stems. Strengthen any weaker stems in the same way, which might not hold the bouquet securely upright.

ASSEMBLY

2 Start by arranging the flowers in your left hand (if you are right-handed!), ensuring that you have a good mix of the different sized roses. Hold the bouquet gently but firmly. Carefully insert the blood lily stems into the bouquet, leaving these delicate flowers proud of the roses; if you pull them among the roses you will break off the very delicate petals. Encircle the roses and blood lilies with the vine leaf stems.

3 Use the nile green tape to cover the binding wire. Trim the stems to the same length after you have spread the wires sufficiently for the bouquet to stand firmly. If you want to include a vase with this bouquet, weigh it down with glass floristry beads to hold it firm. It is not necessary to use a vase, but it does make the whole bouquet more stable.

4 The bouquet may be left in the vase, without the addition of the orange tissue paper, but if you are giving the bouquet to someone as a present it will make a more attractive display if it is wrapped in tissue paper. You may choose to do this over the vase or leave the vase out altogether.

5 Cross the two sheets of tissue paper so that you have eight points visible. Stand the bouquet in the centre and gently enclose the stems, creasing the paper as little as possible. Fasten orange organza ribbon around the elasticized cord, tying it into a voluptuous bow. Trim the ends of the ribbon with a sharp pair of scissors.

'BREATH OF LIFE'

Each of the 'Breath of Life' roses has 25 petals and every petal is a slightly different shape. To make it easier I have used standard rose petal cutters (rather than the 25 templates which would otherwise be needed) but have worked the edges of all the petals strongly to give them more interesting shapes. There is a layer of shorter, paler petals behind the largest petals, which is most noticeable when looking at the half roses. The sepals are short and reflexed. I have not made the leaves to accompany this rose in the hand-tied bouquet, they are mid- to dark green in colour and quite glossy.

Materials

Pale peach and pale green flowerpaste (gum paste)

26- and 18-gauge wires

Cornflour (cornstarch)

Lemon, nasturtium, vine green, holly/ivy and chestnut petal dusts

White bridal satin dust

Fine seedhead stamens

Equipment

Rose petal cutters (TT549, 550, 551, 276)

Very large rose petal veiner (GI)

Silk veining tool (HP)

Papier mâché apricot and apple trays

Nile green floristry tape

Smooth porcelain tool (HP)

Rose calyx cutter (OP R11)

Non-toxic hi-tack glue

CONES

1 Take a medium sized piece of peach flowerpaste. Roll it into a ball and shape it into a fairly short, bulbous cone able to fit within the smallest cutter. Hook the end of a half-length l8-gauge wire, moisten and push it into the base of the cone. Fasten onto the wire and set aside to dry completely.

BUDS

2 Roll out a quantity of the pale peach flowerpaste. Use the smallest petal cutter and cut out a selection of three or five petals (depending upon the size of the bud). Soften the edges with a metal ball tool. Attach the petals to the cone. On some cones spiral three petals, on others all five. Roll back the edges of some of the petals slightly, others more strongly. On some centres add a fourth petal to ensure added interest. Make sure that the cone is not visible.

3 Cut a 26-gauge wire into five, making a small hook at one end of each piece of wire. Roll out a piece of the paste into a long sausage then roll it out again to leave a thicker ridge of paste. Cut out three petals using cutter TT551, positioning the point over the thick ridge. Moisten the hook with egg white and insert it into the point. Dust the rose petal veiner with cornflour and vein the petals. Soften the edges of the petals on a non-stick board using the silk veining tool. Work the edges of the petals strongly with the frilling tool over the side of your finger. Place the petals to dry in apricot trays in order to cup them. The edges of these petals are strongly frilled.

4 Repeat this process once again, this time cutting five petals with the same cutter. Vein the petals as before. The edge of these petals are worked as before, but are not as strongly frilled. This time do not place all the petals over the edge of the apricot trays, so that some curve outwards and some do not. Use the smooth porcelain tool to curl the edges of the petals.

COLOURING AND ASSEMBLING THE BUDS

5 Dust the petals on the cones with nasturtium dust, starting just below the top edge of the petals and tapering the colour as you approach the wire. Add lemon yellow to the base of the petals. The strongest colouring is in the centre of each petal.

6 Dust the base of each wired petal with lemon yellow petal dust near the wire (inside and out). Leave some yellow visible on the inside of the petal and overdust with nasturtium, tapering the colour as it reaches the edge of the petal. Leave the edge undusted. The back of the petal can be left paler than the inside, just flushing the petals with a little nasturtium.

7 Tape the petals to the cone using half-width nile green floristry tape. Some buds will have just three wired petals, some five and some eight. Arrange the petals on each rose attractively.

CALYX

8 Roll a ball of paste into a cone, pinch out the thick end of the cone into a circle. Place this on your board and roll out the paste until thin using your medium celstick. Cut out the calyx. Soften the edges of the sepals on your foam pad using a metal ball tool. Mark a groove down the centre of each sepal. Use sharp scissors to cut fine hairs onto the edges of the sepals. Use the back of a medium celstick to make a hollow in the centre of the calyx.

9 Dust the inside of the calyx with the bridal satin dust and dust the centre of the back of the sepals with some holly/ivy petal dust.

10 Moisten the centre of the calyx and fasten it to the base of the dried buds. The sepals are turned down fairly soon after the bud opens.

HALF ROSE

11 To make the half rose, follow the steps for the bud and add two extra layers of petals. The first layer, which enlarges the bud, is made by using the cutter TT550. To finish the half rose, add another layer of five petals, fastened behind the large petals. These petals are also wired but are cut using the smallest cutter TT276.

12 Dust the small petals mainly with the lemon yellow dust, using only a small amount of nasturtium. They should be a lot paler than the larger petals. Form the calyx as described above.

FULL ROSE CENTRE

13 Attach a small ball of pale green paste to a hooked, moistened, 18-gauge wire. Flatten the top. Cut the filaments of a number of stamens very short and insert them into the paste, completely covering it. Set aside until dry. Cut off longer lengths of stamens and then attach them to the wire below the dried centre with a little non-toxic hi-tack glue. These stamens should protrude above those that are set into the flowerpaste. Neaten the base of the stamens by trimming off the untidy pieces of filament. Tape with nile green floristry tape.

14 Dust the stamens first with the yellow petal dust and then with some chestnut. The chestnut colouring should be stronger on the outer stamens.

15 Cut out five petals with the TT276 and vein them with the rose petal veiner. Mark a line strongly down the centre of each petal using a dresden tool. Work the edges first with the silk veining tool and then with the frilling tool. Place in apricot trays to set.

16 Make five petals each with the TT549, TT551, TT550 cutters and another set of five petals made with the TT276, but this time do not mark the petals with the dresden tool. The edges of the petals are worked as before, curling back the edges of the larger petals attractively with the smooth porcelain tool. Set in the papier mâché apple trays to dry, ensuring the curved back petals are arranged over the edges of the apple cups. Dust the petals, making the inside of each petal darker than the outside, and the edge of each petal pale. The outer set of TT276 petals are quite yellow and pale as described above.

ASSEMBLING THE FULL ROSE

17 Tape the first set of small petals around the centre, then add the petals in increasing sizes, ensuring the petals of each succeeding layer are arranged across the join of the previous layer. Finish with the small, pale layer of petals. Make the calyx as before. After completing all the rosebuds, half roses and full roses, steam them lightly to set the petal dust.

VINE LEAVES

These are very useful and attractive leaves to use for backing arrangements. When my younger daughter got married, I incorporated both vine and hop leaves into the floral decoration, as she enjoys wine and my son-in-law likes a glass or two of beer.

Materials

- Pale green flowerpaste (gum paste)
- 28-, 26-, 24- and 22-gauge wires
- Cornflour (cornstarch)
- Vine green, holly/ivy, moss, forest green and chestnut petal dusts

Equipment

- Vine leaf cutters (J)
- Vine leaf veiners (GI)
- Dimpled foam
- Nile green floristry tape

1 Roll out a piece of pale green paste over a groove in your board (select the size of groove suitable for the size of leaf). A pale line of paste will become visible in the groove.

2 Moisten the wire and place it along the pale ridge, rolling over the wire with a pin to embed it into the ridge. Fold back the paste that extends above the wire down to the edge of the board, sandwiching the wire between two layers of paste. Roll out the paste once again. Cut out the leaf shape and soften the edges with a metal ball tool.

3 Dust the veiner with a little cornflour, then place the wire very carefully down the central vein and vein the leaf. Place onto dimpled foam to dry in an attractive shape.

4 It is best to dust the leaves before they are completely dry (they should be holding their shape). Dust a little vine green on one side of the leaves and then overdust with holly/ivy. Dust a bit of chestnut along the edges of the leaves and then overdust with moss green. Steam the leaves lightly to set the dust once they are completely hard.

5 Repeat for the other leaves, varying the wire gauge as appropriate.

6 Tape a selection of leaves onto a 22-gauge wire to create a stem of vine leaves. Arrange the leaves alternately.

Blood Lilies

(*Haemanthus katherinae*)

Haemanthus is a South African genus that grows in large umbels with the buds very tightly packed in the centre. The flowers in this genus range from bright scarlet through coral-red to peachy orange and white. The particular variety I have used is called 'Roi d'Albert', chosen for its especially prominent stamens.

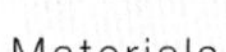

Materials

30- and 24-gauge white wires

Pale apricot, pale yellow and pale green flowerpaste (gum paste)

Red, holly/ivy green and lemon yellow petal dusts

Equipment

Nile green floristry tape

3.5cm (1¼in) *Agapanthus* cutter

PISTIL

1 To make the pistil (the female part), you will first need to moisten the top of a half-length 24-gauge wire. Then thread a small piece of pale apricot flowerpaste onto the wire and work it on until it is very fine – the pistil should ultimately be about 4cm (1½in long). Once complete, bend it into a soft S-shaped curve.

STAMENS

2 For the stamens, cut 30-gauge wires into one-third lengths. Then take a small piece of pale apricot flowerpaste and thread it onto a moistened wire. Work the paste onto the wire until it is very

slender, aiming for a length of about 4cm (1½in). Curve gently.

ANTHER

3 To make the male organ of the flower, first take a tiny piece of pale yellow flowerpaste and roll it into the shape of a grain to form the anther. Use the veiner end of a dresden tool to mark a dent into the anther and curve the anther gently backwards. Moisten the tip of the covered filament and attach the anther to the filament.

ASSEMBLING AND COLOURING THE CENTRE

4 Tape each of the six stamens around the pistil with some nile green floristry tape, cutting off any excess wire using a pair of wire cutters.

5 Using dusting brushes, dust the anther with a little of the lemon yellow petal dust and then dust the filaments with the red petal dust.

PETALS

6 Roll out a piece of apricot flowerpaste into a ball and then form it into a cone. Roll the cone out further to create a long, slender throat and pinch the thick end flat.

7 Place the flat circle on your board and roll out the paste from the throat, making sure it is slender enough to fit through the centre of the cutter. Then position the *Agapanthus* cutter over the throat and cut out the shape of the petals. You will need to make sure that the flat circle of flowerpaste is wider than the 3.5cm (1¼in) width of the *Agapanthus* cutter.

8 Place the petals on the foam pad and soften the edges gently with a metal ball tool, being careful not to distort the petals. Vein strongly down the centre of each petal from the back of the petals.

ASSEMBLING AND COLOURING THE FLOWER

9 Make a hollow in the centre of the flower with a large celstick. The hollow should be large enough to accommodate the taped stamens and pistil.

10 Moisten the base of the pistil and stamens and then pull the centre into the hollow in the centre of the flower, ensuring that the stamens meet the veined centre of each petal. Repeat the process for the other flowers, pulling the centre into the hollow of each petal.

11 Gently curve the petals towards the stamens, taking special care not to distort the backward cupping of the individual petals.

HIP (OVARY)

12 Roll a very small ball of green flowerpaste onto the base of the throat to make a hip. Moisten and attach the hip to the flower, making sure that no joins can be seen.

FINAL TOUCHES

13 Dust the throat with some red petal dust, making it a deeper colour near the hip. Dust the hip with holly/ivy green. Steam the flower to set the dust. A little sheen on this flower would be helpful so steam it for a second time. Attractively arrange the stamens.

BUDS

14 I have chosen not to use the buds of the blood lily in this arrangement. These buds are about 2cm (¾in) long with a slender throat that also includes a hip. The necks are not as long as those of the flowers, and the bud and throat are shaped into a graceful curve. Mark three petals on the bud. Half open flowers would have three petals still curving inwards quite strongly.

I designed this cake to celebrate my parents' Coral anniversary. The floral posy has been tied with two different types of florists' wire to create a sea urchin styled centrepiece. The starfish, sea horse and shell design on the cake echoes the sea theme, with the roses only just touching upon the coral theme. *–Alan*

Starfish and Coral

Cake and Decoration

20cm (8in) heart-shaped cake and board
Apricot glaze
1kg (2¼lb) white almond paste (marzipan)
Clear alcohol (kirsch or Cointreau)
1.5kg (3⅓lb) white sugarpaste (cold rolled fondant)
Fine and broad naked ribbon
Royal icing
Apricot, vine green, holly/ivy and bridal satin petal dusts
Florists' wire covered in beige paper
Fine silver crimped reel wire
Small amount of flowerpaste (gum paste)

Flowers

4 full 'Peppermint' roses
4 half 'Peppermint' roses
5 'Peppermint' rosebuds
8 beetleweed leaves
6 eucalyptus leaves
Bear grass

Equipment

Non-toxic glue stick
Sea-life cutter-veiners (FMM)
33cm (13in) round base glass stand with diamond shaped cut glass support
Florists' staysoft
Nile green floristry tape

PREPARATION

1 Brush the cake with apricot glaze, cover with almond paste and allow to dry. Moisten the almond paste and cover cake and board with sugarpaste. Transfer cake to board. Leave to dry. Attach the fine ribbon to the cake base with royal icing. Attach the broad ribbon to the board edge with the non-toxic glue stick.

2 Roll out white flowerpaste until thin and cut out the sea horse, shell and starfish shapes. Dust with apricot and bridal satin. Then add a touch of vine green and holly/ivy dust also mixed with bridal satin. Attach pieces to the cake before they have dried so that the shapes can be given some movement. Position the cake on top of the glass base stand and add a tilt to the cake with balls of florists' staysoft.

ASSEMBLING THE SPRAYS

3 Position the larger roses at the centre then tape half roses and rosebuds around the outside of the posy shape. Add the beetleweed foliage to the edges and tape them in tightly.

4 Form a cage around the posy with florists' wire covered in beige paper. Curve each of the 'bars' as you go and offset the centre point where all the wires meet. Next add some detail weaving using the silver crimped wire. Repeat for a single rose, surrounding it with eucalyptus leaves.

5 Next use the paper covered wire to create a series of long, connecting waves. Tape the two sprays onto either end of the wire lengths. Position the larger spray at an angle on top of the cake and the smaller on the glass base.

6 Cut out a few extra starfish shapes, dust as before and then position on top of the wires, using a tiny amount of softened flowerpaste to hold them in place. Soften the flowerpaste with egg white to the consistency of royal icing.

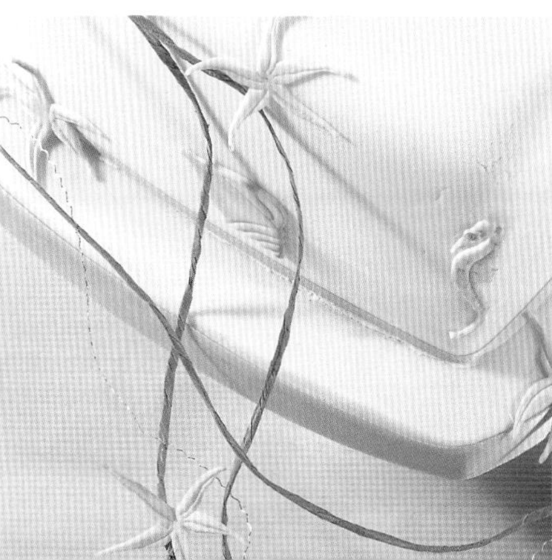

'PEPPERMINT' (QUICK ROSE)

To create the 'Peppermint' rose I have employed the 'quick rose' method. Often known as the 'all-in-one' rose it does actually produce a very pretty flower. Time is saved in the cutting out process as each layer is made up from one five-petal blossom shape. This is a very good rose for people who want to produce a large quantity of small- or medium-sized roses. Once you have made your quick rose, it can easily be coloured with the distinctive green-tinged petal edges of the 'Peppermint' rose. To make a successful quick rose, keep the petals in a fairly tight formation to begin with and keep each pair of petals either the same height or slightly higher than the previous two.

Materials

Pale bitterlemon and mid-holly/ivy flowerpaste (gum paste)

26-, 24-, 20- and 18-gauge wires

Apricot, plum, white, primrose, vine green, moss, forest and holly/ivy petal dusts

Equipment

Large five-petal blossom cutter (OP/J/TT or template page 156)

Sharp scalpel or sharp, fine scissors

Rose calyx cutter (size will depend upon blossom cutter used for rose) (OP)

Nile green floristry tape

PREPARATION

1 Roll a ball of well kneaded white flowerpaste into a cone shape with a sharp point (there is no point in using coloured paste for this base cone as it will not be visible in the finished flower). The cone should be smaller than one of the petals in the blossom shape.

2 Bend a large open hook in the end of an 18-gauge wire, moisten the end and insert the wire into the broad end of the cone. Make sure that the hook is inserted almost to the tip of the cone shape, pinching the paste from the base of the cone around the wire to secure it into place. Allow to dry completely.

FIRST LAYER

3 Grease your work board with white fat and then remove the excess with kitchen paper to both clean and condition the board. This will stop the paste sticking to the work board. You must not leave too much fat on the board as this will make the finished work look greasy.

4 Take well-kneaded pale bitter lemon flowerpaste and roll it out quite thin. Cut out a blossom shape using an all-in-one blossom cutter or the template. Remove the shape from the cutter and place it onto a pad. If you are using a metal cutter then you will need to make a cut between each of the petals using either a sharp scalpel or a pair of fine, sharp scissors.

5 Soften the edges of each of the petals using a metal ball tool or the rounded end of a large celstick, working half on the edge of the petal and half on the pad. Do not try to frill the petals too much as you only need to thin and remove the harsh cut edges afterwards.

6 Moisten one of the petals with fresh egg white and then insert the wired rose cone through the centre of the blossom shape. Support the paste from behind with your fingers. Now position the cone onto the moistened petal so that the petal stands about 0.5cm (¼in) above the cone. Tuck in the left-hand side of the petal tightly so that it starts to form a spiral shape. Then tightly wrap the right-hand side around to form a complete spiral, making sure that the tip of the cone is completely hidden.

7 Next, moisten the opposite petal and position over the first petal, pressing down the right-hand side of the petal firmly. Then moisten the petal opposite that one and tuck the right-hand side underneath the previous petal to form an 'S' shape. Once you have positioned the petals correctly, tighten them to form a neat centre.

8 Repeat the process with the last two petals, which should also be opposites. Try to pull down on each petal at an angle. Do not be tempted simply to wrap each of the petals around the cone as this will just cause the rose centre to be opened up too quickly.

BUDS

9 If you are using rosebuds in the spray, turn back the edges of the last two petals on this layer and add a calyx, made from the mid-holly/ivy paste, as for the 'Golden Wings' rose on page 24.

SECOND LAYER

10 Roll out some more flowerpaste and cut out another five-petal blossom shape. Soften the edges as before and then cup the centre of each petal using either the ball tool or the rounded end of the celstick.

11 Moisten the edges of each of the petals and then thread the blossom shape through the first stage of the rose, so that the petals of the second layer touch the base of the first. Line up the petals so that the first petal overlaps the join in the previous layer. Spiral two of the petals together, again keeping them at either the same height or slightly higher. Roll back their side edges. You might also like to pinch a slight central vein to the petals at this stage too.

12 Next, position the remaining three petals, following a much more relaxed spiral shape. Curl back the edges of each of the petals and also pinch a vein if required. The edges of two of the petals should be curled more to create an almost collar effect. This stage is termed a half rose.

THIRD LAYER

13 Roll out more paste, cut and work on the blossom shape as before. Make the cupping shape a little stronger this time. Use a dresden veining tool to vein the centre of each petal gently.

14 Moisten the centre of the blossom shape and the 'V' shape at the base of each petal. Thread through the half rose and position the first petal of this last layer over the join between the two collar petals. Pinch either side of the petal at the base to retain the cupped shape. Make sure you do not press at the centre of the petal as this will flatten the petal shape, creating a rose that looks like a cabbage!

15 Next, position the opposite petal, again over a join in the previous layer. Continue to add the remaining three petals in exactly the same way. Curl back the edges to create a more realistic effect.

16 Allow the paste to firm up a little before dusting the rose. To create the 'Peppermint' rose, first dust with a mixture of apricot, plum and white petal dusts mixed together. Try to increase the depth of colour at the very heart of the rose to create a focal point to the flower. Then to create the distinctive 'peppermint' colouring dust the edges with a mixture of vine and moss green. A touch of primrose mixed with white added to the base of each petal helps to lend a glow to the rose.

17 Add a calyx as for the 'Golden Wings' rose on page 24. Dust the calyx with forest green and then overdust with holly/ivy petal dust. Steam the flower to set the colour and to remove the very dry and dusted appearance.

LEAVES

18 Refer to the instructions on page 24 for making leaves for the 'Golden Wings' rose, using mid-holly/ivy flowerpaste.

NOTE

If you have to make a few roses in a hurry and do not have any pre-dried centres, try the following method:
Hook the end of the 20- or 18-gauge wire, make the cone as before and then heat the hook over a naked flame (lighter or hob) until it is red hot. Quickly insert the hook into the base of the cone, neaten the base and allow it to cool and firm a little. The sugar caramelizes, cools quickly and gives a secure base that can be worked on straight away.

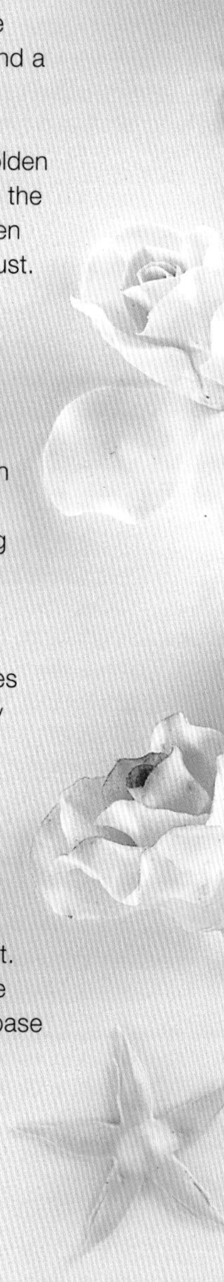

BEETLEWEED (*Galax viceolata*) AND BEAR GRASS (*Xerophyllum tenax*)

The curious leaves of the beetleweed can be used either flat or rolled up. I have scaled down the size of the leaves to use with the roses in this book. Bear grass is an essential foliage for the florist when line emphasis is required in an arrangement.

BEETLEWEED

Materials

Mid-holly/ivy flowerpaste (gum paste)

Red, aubergine, holly/ivy, forest and moss green petal dusts

Half glaze

Equipment

Leaf template (see page 156)

Plain-edged cutting wheel (PME)

24 and 22-gauge white wires

Serrated cutting tool (AP)

Large nasturtium leaf veiner (GI)

Nile green floristry tape

BEAR GRASS

Materials

Forest and holly/ivy petal dusts

Half glaze (optional)

Equipment

28- or 26-gauge wires

Nile green floristry tape

BEETLEWEED

1 Roll out some green flowerpaste, leaving a thick ridge for the wire. Cut out the leaf shape from the template, employing a free-hand method and using the plain-edged cutting wheel. Insert a moistened wire into the thick ridge.

2 To create the serrated edge to the leaf, use the serrated cutting tool to bite at the edges of the leaf. Use the broad end of a dresden tool to flatten and elongate some of the serrations.

3 Vein the leaf with the nasturtium leaf veiner. You will need to use the veiner upside down. When making nasturtium leaves, the veins are prominent under the leaf; with beetleweed, the veins are prominent on the leaf's upper surface.

4 Soften the edges of the leaf with a metal ball tool. Pinch the central vein firmly. Dry the leaves flat or roll them up as required for the piece you are working on.

5 Dust the edges of each leaf with a mixture of red and aubergine and then overdust with forest green, moss and holly/ivy petal dusts. Dip into a half glaze and allow to dry.

BEAR GRASS

1 Tape together one, two or three long lengths of wire alongside one another using half-width nile green floristry tape. Flatten the taped wires with a rolling pin. Trim the tip of the grass into a point.

2 Dust with the various green petal dusts and glaze if required. Give the whole length of the grass a graceful curve or use as required.

These two stylish arrangements offer further ideas for competition pieces. The green vase arrangement (right) relies heavily on line and curve created by the straight lines of the bottle, silver mesh and rosebud stems and the graceful curves and twists of the bear grass and beetleweed (page 121). The rosebuds are made using the 'quick' method (pages 118–20) and the petals are very lightly dusted with plum dust. In the exotic arrangement blow, two gymea lilies (pages 132–3) have been arranged in a shallow glass candleholder with a few red 'Massai' rosebuds (pages 126–7), red chillies (see *Exotic Sugar Flowers for Cakes*, pages 144–5) and crocosmia berries (page 143) used as filler flowers.

Contemporary Arrangements

Red roses make an ideal focal flower for a wedding theme and, combined with berries and stark twisting stems, a stunning effect can be achieved to complement a winter setting. The trailing stems of Oriental bittersweet lend this bouquet an almost freestyle shape in the form of a Hogarth curve. –*Alan*

Winter Wedding

Flowers

1 full 'Massai' rose

2 half 'Massai' roses

2 'Massai' rosebuds

11 *Rosa rugosa* hips (see page 18)

3 trailing stems of Oriental climbing bittersweet

9 sets of rose leaves

Materials and Equipment

18-gauge wire

Nile green and brown floristry tape

Fine-nosed pliers

Red or green velvet ribbon to trim bouquet handle

PREPARATION

1 First of all, tape 18-gauge wire onto any of the flower stems that may need strengthening, using half- or even full-width nile green floristry tape. If any of the bittersweet stems need to be elongated, this can be done by taping around the stems with brown tape.

ASSEMBLY

2 Taking the two longest stems of Oriental bittersweet, form the basic outline of the bouquet by bending each stem to a 90° angle and then taping them together.

3 Next, place the full rose in the central position of the bouquet. Make sure this focal flower stands slightly proud of all the other flowers as you build up the bouquet. Fill in around the main rose with the two rosebuds and two half roses. Use fine-nosed pliers to position each flower carefully into the bouquet. At this stage I usually tape round the stems with full-width floristry tape.

4 Add the rose hips in groups to fill in the remaining spaces between the roses, and add an extra stem of bittersweet to create the complete width of the bouquet.

5 Finally, add the rose leaves to the bouquet, positioning two longer leaf stems to follow the curve of the two longer bittersweet stems that started off the bouquet. Trim off any excess wire and tape neatly over the top.

6 If you are entering a competition with a bridal bouquet, it is important to produce a neat finish for the back handle using a broad ribbon. Pin the ribbon at the top of the handle, then carefully wrap the ribbon around the handle and back up to the top again. Insert another pin to hold it in place. Florists will often use separate leaves to hide the mechanics at the back of a bouquet. If you are adding these extra leaves, ensure that the leaves are seen face up when the back is in view.

'Massai'

This red rose is based on a florists' hybrid rose called 'Massai'. The centre of the rose has been made with a layer of five petals, all interlinked with one another. The secret to achieving good colouring with a red rose is to dust the flower before it has had a chance to dry completely. Red roses are always a favourite choice for wedding bouquets and, of course, for Valentine's Day!

Materials

18-gauge wire

White, Christmas red/ruby and holly/ivy flowerpaste (gum paste)

Christmas red and ruby paste colouring

Red, ruby, aubergine, holly/ivy and forest green petal dusts

Equipment

Fine-nosed pliers

Pale green floristry tape

Rose petal cutters (TT551, 550)

Very large rose petal veiner (GI)

Rose calyx cutters (OP R11b)

CONE

1 Tape over an 18-gauge wire and bend a large open hook in the end using pliers. Form a cone shape using some well-kneaded white flowerpaste. Make sure the tip is quite pointed and the base fairly broad. Moisten the hooked wire and insert it into the broad end of the cone. Push the wire closer towards the point of the bud so that it is well secured. Pinch some of the paste from the base down onto the wire to secure it further. The cone should be no larger than the smallest cutter you are planning to use. You will need to make some cone shapes slightly smaller with a finer point if you are planning to make rosebuds. Allow to dry overnight if possible.

2 Colour some flowerpaste with a mixture of Christmas red and ruby paste colouring. I tend not to make the base colour as strong as I want the finished flower to be. Red paste can be sticky and difficult to handle and if the depth of red is too strong, then the petal dust finish will not show up and the finished flower may look very dead and flat.

FIRST LAYER

3 Roll out some coloured paste quite thinly and cut out five rose petal shapes using the smaller cutter (TT551). Place the petals onto a pad and soften the edges using either a medium metal ball tool or the rounded end of a large celstick, working half on the edge of the petal and half on the pad or your hand.

4 Place each petal in turn into the very large double-sided rose petal veiner. You will need to press very firmly to make a good, deep impression. When you have all five petals veined, moisten each of them with fresh egg white. Place the first petal onto the dried wired rose cone, leaving about 0.5cm (¼in) of the petal above the tip of the cone. Tuck the left-hand side of the petal in towards

the cone, trying to hide the tip of the white cone underneath. Tuck the next petal tightly into the first and then repeat with the remaining petals until you have a tightly interlinked and spiralled centre. Tighten all of the petals down, pulling them at an angle to the base. Leave one of the petals open ready to take the first petal of the next layer.

SECOND LAYER

5 Cut out another five petals using the same sized rose petal cutter as before. Vein and soften the petals as described above. Tuck the first petal underneath the open petal from the previous layer. Close the last petal from the first layer on top of this petal. Place the next petal over the join. Repeat with the remaining petals, working around the rose until you get to the last petal, which will need to be tucked underneath the first of this layer. Pinch the centre of each petal slightly between your finger and thumb to give a central vein. Once again, keep one of the petal edges open to take the first petal of the next layer.

6 If you are making buds then you should have a tightly spiralled rose at this stage. Curl back all of the edges gently and add a calyx.

THIRD LAYER

7 Repeat the process again using the same sized cutter as the previous two layers. Start to open up the rose shape a little more this time and don't forget to pinch the petals again.

FOURTH AND FIFTH LAYERS

8 Roll out some more red paste. Cut out ten petals using the largest cutter (TT550). Soften and vein the petals as before. This time you will need to cup the centre of each petal either with a metal ball tool or by working the centre between your fingers and thumbs. Moisten the base of five of the petals and attach them in turn opposite one another, placing each over a join in the previous layer or in the layer you are creating as you work. Curl back the edges very slightly. Add the remaining five in exactly the same way, but this time curl the edges back a lot more as this is the last layer. Allow to set a little before dusting but do not allow to dry completely.

DUSTING

9 Dust the rose heavily with red and ruby petal dust. Start at the centre of the rose with quite heavy, almost stabbing movements with the brush. Add a touch of aubergine petal dust at the centre of the rose to create more of a focal point. Catch the edges of all of the petals very gently with aubergine, and then, using a slightly smaller brush, dust the base of each petal to create depth within the flower.

10 Allow the flower to dry. If you are trying to achieve a very velvety rose then you will need to steam the flower and re-dust using the same colours.

CALYX AND LEAVES

11 To make the calyx and leaves, refer to the instructions for the 'Elegance' rose on pages 105–6.

12 Finally, add the calyx. Dust the calyx with holly/ivy and forest green petal dusts. With a red rose, I often add some red detail to the tips and edges of the sepals too. If you wish, paint the calyx with quarter glaze to lend it an authentic shine.

Oriental Climbing Bittersweet (*Celastrus*)

I have chosen to use the Asian species of climbing bittersweet, which has a small number of berries in each group. The plant climbs and scrambles by twining itself around trees, shrubs and fences. I like to use them in both autumn and winter floral arrangements.

Materials

- 26- and 20-gauge wires
- Christmas red and cream flowerpaste (gum paste)
- Christmas red colouring
- Fine stamens (optional)
- Red, ruby, cream, nutkin brown and holly/ivy petal dusts
- Full glaze

Equipment

- Fine-nosed pliers
- Sharp scalpel
- Small rose petal cutter (optional)
- Tweezers
- Brown floristry tape
- Paintbrush
- Non-toxic hi-tack glue

BERRIES

1 Bend a large open hook in the end of a 26-gauge wire with fine-nosed pliers. Roll a ball of Christmas red coloured paste, moisten the wire with fresh egg white and insert it into the ball. Pinch the base of the ball onto the wire very slightly to secure the two together.

2 Divide the surface of the berry into three sections using a sharp scalpel. Insert a fine stamen with its tip removed into the centre of the berry (this is optional!). Repeat to make the required number of berries.

3 Dust with red and ruby petal dusts and allow to dry. Dip into a full glaze, shake off the excess and allow to dry. Repeat the glazing process again if you wish to make a very high gloss.

BRACTS

4 The bracts can either be cut out with a small rose petal cutter or hand modelled. Roll a ball of cream paste into a cone shape. Flatten slightly, and then thin the edges of the shape using a small metal ball tool. Try to leave a ridge at the centre of the bract. Pinch the ridge with tweezers or your finger and thumb to emphasize it. Repeat to make three bracts for each berry. Attach to the base of the berry with, what I call, 'gunge' (flowerpaste softened with egg white to make a thick glue). Dust with cream, nutkin brown and a touch of holly/ivy.

ASSEMBLY

5 Tape over a length of 26-gauge wire with brown floristry tape, and then curl it around a paintbrush very gently to create a twisted tendril. Add further, finer tendrils using only floristry tape twisted back onto itself. Add this to a 20-gauge wire. Add a single or a group of berries at the join. Continue until you have the required stem length. Dust the stem with nutkin brown petal dust. Seal the colour if you wish with a non-toxic hi-tack glue, which will dry clear and shiny. If you are feeling guilty about using glue with your sugarwork, just remember that floristry tape has a glue in its make up!

Hand-tied bouquet: This bouquet contains roses from each of the authors. The large focal rose, supplied by Tombi, is based on a hybrid (follow instructions for 'Elegance', pages 104–6). Tony provided the 'Painter' roses that surround the main flower (pages 80–83), and Alan supplied the 'Massai' roses (pages 126-7) and *Rosa rugosa* hips (page 18). The flowers and foliage have been tied into a large round bouquet (see instructions on page 108).

The Handel's Messiah rose is actually a fictional flower of my own creation. I felt the real rose, 'Handel', would be ideal for the arrangement, but the colouring was not right to go with the gymea lilies. I turned a white rose into a red-tinged rose by edging the petals with red and deep magenta dust. *–Tombi*

HANDEL'S MESSIAH

Flowers

- 3 full Handel's Messiah roses
- 3 half Handel's Messiah roses
- 2 Handel's Messiah rosebuds
- 4 gymea lilies
- 2 stems of white ginger
- 6 stems of watsonia
- 5 stems of vine leaves (see page 113)
- 8 stems of small-leaved ruscus (see page 96)

Materials and Equipment

- Red and deep magenta craft dust
- Florists' glass beads or staysoft
- 18-gauge wire
- Nile green floristry tape

ROSES

1 I have used the 'Elegance' rose to form the basic flower for my imaginary, red-edged creation; the instructions for making this rose are on pages 104–6. Follow these instructions up to and including the dusting of the petals with the yellow and green craft dusts.

2 Now use the red and deep magenta craft dust very carefully to dust the edge of each of the petals (this same dust will be used to colour the gymea lilies). Great care needs to be taken when applying these colours as they are extremely powerful and if they touch the petal in the wrong place it will show when the flower is steamed. So be sure to use a very small amount of colour on your brush and apply the colour slowly and carefully.

3 Having achieved the desired effect, the next step is to assemble the rose and add the calyx. For this you can resume the method described for the 'Elegance' rose. You will need to steam the roses in order to set the dust, before adding them to the arrangement.

4 Instructions can be found on page 96 for making the small-leaved ruscus and on page 113 for making the vine leaves.

ASSEMBLY

5 Fill your chosen vase with either florists' glass beads or staysoft. Place all the flower and foliage elements in readiness, elongating and strengthening with tape and wire as necessary.

6 Put the ruscus stems in place first of all. Then add the white ginger flowers.

7 Add watsonia buds and flowers where they form part of the outer shape of the arrangement. Then position the full and half roses and rosebuds as shown.

8 Finally, use the gymea lilies to recess between the roses and add vine leaf stems to broaden out the overall shape of your display.

Gymea Lily

Gymea lilies come from Australia. They are very large, ugly looking plants which are similar to South African aloes in shape. Their buds open to reveal attractive flowers. Several varieties of gymea lilies work very well in bridal bouquets where you need to add interesting shape and colour to enhance the bouquet. I first came across gymea lilies in a bridal magazine and was then lucky to see them 'in the flesh' at the Interflora Exhibition held at the Design Centre in London.

Materials

Pale pink, red and pale green flowerpaste (gum paste)

28-, 24- and 20-gauge white wires

Red and deep magenta craft dusts

Holly/ivy and vine green petal dusts

Equipment

Six-petal blossom cutter (OP N2)

Long leaf cutter (TT666)

Medium veiner from the Amaryllis set (GI)

Nile green floristry tape

PISTIL

1 Make the pistil by attaching a small piece of paste to a moistened half-length of 24-gauge wire. Form the paste into a small bulb then dust with a mixture of the red and deep magenta craft dusts and set aside.

FLOWER CENTRE

2 Roll out a piece of red flowerpaste into the shape of a cone. Pinch out the broad base and roll into a circle. The paste should not be rolled too thinly. Cut out a shape using the six-petal blossom cutter. Use a large celstick to make a hollow in the centre of the shape. Pinch half the length of each

petal into a tube. Flatten the lower half of each petal between your finger and thumb. The effect you should be trying to achieve is rather like that of a neck emerging from a person's shoulders.

3 Use the veiner end of a dresden tool to mark an indentation from the centre of the cone to where the petal has been formed into a tube.

4 Next moisten the pistil and pull it through the centre. The pistil should be approximately 1.25cm (½in) taller than the tubular centre petals.

5 Dust the centre with red and then deep magenta craft dusts. Allow to dry. Steam to set the dust.

ANTHERS

6 Roll out small pieces of the pale green flowerpaste into carrot shapes. Then vein them down the centre with the veiner end of a dresden tool.

7 Moisten the broad end of each of the carrots and stick them very carefully to the tubular petals. The green anthers should be arranged to point towards the pistil. The pistil should protrude above the anthers. Set aside to dry. Very carefully dust with a little vine and holly/ivy green petal dust.

OUTER PETALS

8 Roll out pale pink paste on a groove in your board. Moisten a 28-gauge wire and place along the pale line of the groove. Sandwich the wire between two layers of paste. The wire should extend almost to the tip of the petal. Cut six petals with the long leaf cutter, using two-thirds of the length of the cutter. Neaten the base of the petal with fine scissors.

9 Place on the veiner and vein the petal. Then place the petal on a foam pad. Use the small end of a metal ball tool to cup the tip of the petal inwards and mark a vein down the centre with the veiner end of a dresden tool.

10 If this petal is to form part of a partly open flower then you will need to curve the wire inwards. If it is to form part of an open flower, curve the petal backwards, retaining the vein down the centre of the petal and keeping the tip hooked. Set aside to harden.

11 Before the paste is dry, very carefully dust the back of the petals with the red and deep magenta dust. Set aside to dry. Make six petals for each flower.

ASSEMBLING THE FLOWER

12 Tape the six petals around the centre with nile green floristry tape, ensuring the petals are well bedded in the tape and no wire is visible.

13 At this point, form the pedicel by taking a piece of red paste and working it onto the wire. Use a moistened finger to neaten the junction between the petals and the pedicel. Dust the pedicel with a mixture of red and magenta dust. Arrange the petals in their correct position and set to dry. Steam the flower to set the dust and allow to dry.

14 Take a small ball of pale green paste, attach it to the base of the pedicel. Dust lightly with vine green and holly/ivy dust. Steam and allow to set.

White Watsonia

This is an attractive South African flower that comes in several colours, on this occasion I have chosen the white watsonia.

Materials

White flowerpaste (gum paste)
30-, 28- and 20-gauge wires
Pale yellow small seedhead stamens
Lemon yellow, vine green and holly/ivy petal dusts

Equipment

Nile green floristry tape
Non-toxic hi-tack glue
Cutters (OP N3, N4 and N5)

1 Take a small piece of paste, roll it into a small cone, moisten the end of a 30-gauge wire and insert it into the pointed end of the cone. Roll the broad end of the cone into a slight point. Mark three grooves onto the bud either with a craft knife or using a cage. Tip the bud forward into a gentle curve. Set aside to dry. Make several buds for each stem of watsonia, increasing the size gradually. The flowers are also made in increasing sizes as they go down the stem.

2 To make the pistil take a piece of quarter-length 28-gauge wire, cut a piece of nile green floristry tape in half using a tape shredder, cut it into three lengthways for about 1.25cm (½in) and then tape onto the wire, leaving the cut tape protruding from the end of the wire. Twist these into strands and trim.

3 Take three pale yellow stamens and cut off the anthers quite short. Using non-toxic hi-tack glue, stick the six filaments around the taped centre, positioning them just below the pistil. Set aside to dry. If you prefer you can tape the stamens in place. Dust the anthers with the lemon yellow dust. Make sufficient centres for all the flowers needed for the arrangement.

4 Take a piece of white paste, roll into a cone. Pinch the broad end into a circle and place this on your board. The pedicel should be fine enough to pass easily through the centre of the cutter. Roll out the circle quite fine using a celstick, then cut out a shape. Place the petals on a foam pad and soften the edges with a ball tool. Using a large celstick, open the throat of the flower. Place the petals back on the foam with the inside of the petals uppermost. Stroke down the centre of each petal with the veiner end of a dresden tool to indent each petal.

5 Insert the centre into the throat of the flower and pull into place. Fasten the flower firmly to the wire, removing any excess paste. The throat should be long and slender. Curve the flower gently before setting aside to dry.

6 Tape about five or six buds onto each stem, then about five flowers in increasing sizes. Dust the base of each flower where it is taped to the stem, first with a dusting of vine green and then a light overdusting of holly/ivy. Steam to set the dust.

White Ginger

The petals on this flower are actually stamenoids: stamens that take on a petal-like shape. To make the instructions easier, I will refer to them as petals and sepals.

Materials

White flowerpaste (gum paste)
30-, 28- and 24-gauge wires
Lemon yellow and vine green petal dusts

Equipment

Nile green and white floristry tape
Sharp scalpel
Cutters (TT225, 733)
Medium veiner from the Amaryllis set (GI)
Silk veining tool (HP)
Dimpled foam

1 Form the cone with white flowerpaste and insert a hooked, one-third length 28-gauge wire. Leave a thickened bulb at the end, making the pedicel long and slender. Roll the thick end to a point. Pinch three ridges onto the bud, pushing tweezers into the paste at the same time to give three ridges with curved broader pieces between them. Make two or three bud sizes. Dust the stem/wire junction with vine green and tape the wire. To form a spray, tape two or three buds together before adding a flower.

2 For the pistil, cut a half-length of 24-gauge wire and attach paste to the moistened tip, working it into a bulbous shape. Divide it in two with a sharp scalpel. Tape the wire with white tape. Measure the wire against the TT733 cutter and bend the wire sharply. Curve the wire above the bend. Roll out paste over a groove, then moisten a one-third length of 28-gauge wire and place it along the groove, about two-thirds the length of cutter TT733. Sandwich the wire and cut out the dorsal petal. Use the 'V' of the cutter to cut out a section at the centre of the top edge of the petal. Neaten the edge into a heart shape. Vein with the veiner, then flute it with the silk veining tool. Pinch to create a strong central vein. Bend the petal backwards. Place on dimpled foam to set. Repeat step 3 using cutter TT225. Position the cutter so that what would normally be the point of the leaf is at the edge of the board, to make a broad front to the petal. Repeat to create an opposing lateral petal. Place in the veiner then work with the silk veining tool so the veins resemble those on the rear petal. For these lateral petals there is a ridge along the centre of the upper surface. Leave to dry on dimpled foam.

3 For the sepals, thread a little paste onto a moistened 30-gauge wire to form a slender, pointed tube. The wire should be almost to the tip of the tube. Use the back of the veiner to flatten the tube. Neaten the edge with scissors. Soften the edges with a ball tool. Pinch to create a central vein and attractively curve the sepal backwards.

4 Fasten the pistil to the back petal with white tape, curving it towards the petal. Tape in the two lateral petals just in front of the dorsal petal, curving away from each other. Add the slender sepals at the petal junctions. Tape down to the base of the wire. Moisten the taped wire below the petals and stamens and work paste onto it to form a pedicel. Smooth the join with a dampened finger. Curve the pedicel forwards. Dust the split bulb at the tip of the pistil with lemon yellow (it should be very pale). Add yellow and vine green at the petals/sepal junction inside the flower. Dust a little vine green where the pedicel meets the wire. Steam to set.

The focal flower in this bouquet is obviously the rose. I have, however, added some orchids, 'Canary creeper', *Crocosmia* seedheads and foliage to the display. Despite the orchids being quite large and colourful, the rose still manages to demand the most attention at the centre of the bouquet. *–Alan*

White Rose & Orchid Bridal Bouquet

Flowers

- 1 full 'Pascali' rose (see page 103)
- 2 half 'Pascali' roses
- 4 'Pascali' rosebuds
- 3 stems of 'Canary creeper'
- 3 Phragmipedium orchids
- 5 stems of *Crocosmia* seedheads
- 3 white *Coelogyne ochracea*
- 4 stems of ruscus (see page 96)
- 5 stems of golden hop leaves

Materials and Equipment

- 18-gauge wire
- Nile green floristry tape
- Fine-nosed pliers
- Wire cutters

For this bridal bouquet all the flowers and foliage have been made from cold porcelain. If, however, the bouquet is to be displayed on a wedding cake rather than being held by the bride or bridesmaids, then they could all be made just as easily from flowerpaste. Cold porcelain is an ideal medium to work in if you want to make a bouquet for a bride to carry.

PREPARATION

1 You will first of all need to strengthen the stems on the larger flowers, and lengthen any with stems that are a little too short, by taping additional 18-gauge wire alongside the main stems with some nile green floristry tape.

ASSEMBLY

2 Tape together the ruscus and golden hop stems to define the outline of the bouquet. Using the pliers, bend each stem at a 90° angle to form a natural-style handle to the bouquet. One of the stems should be longer than the others.

3 Position the largest rose at the centre of the bouquet to form the focal point. Next add the phragmipedium orchids, bending each of their stems to help them sit comfortably in the bouquet. Tape in the three stems of 'Canary creeper'. The longest creeper stem should coincide with the longest stems of ruscus and hop. Add the remaining half roses and rosebuds around the central rose.Tape them in securely with full-width floristry tape, trimming off the excess wires as you go. Add the *Crocosmia* berries to the outline of the bouquet. These will help to soften the edges and give extra definition to the shape. Lastly, add the three *Coelogyne ochracea*, which should be tucked into the gaps around the roses.

NOTE

To form the hop leaves, follow the same instructions for making vine leaves (see page 113), but the leaves should be cut with Hop Leaf cutters (TT) and veined using Hop Leaf veiners (GI).

'Canary Creeper' (*Tropaeolum canariense*)

Although the flowers of this plant are a canary yellow and quite bird-like (being a child of the Seventies they often remind me of Big Bird from Sesame Street!) it is thought that the name refers to the fact that the plant was first introduced to the Canary Islands from their native South America.

Materials

White or pale lemon seedhead stamens

33-, 30- , 28-, 26-, 24- and 22-gauge wires

Primrose, lemon, forest, vine green, white and holly/ivy petal dusts

White, pale lemon and holly/ivy flowerpaste (gum paste)

Nasturtium liquid food colour

Quarter glaze

Equipment

Non-toxic hi-tack glue

Small rose petal cutter (TT278)

Sharp scalpel or fine scissors

Ceramic silk veining tool (HP)

Nile green floristry tape

Rose calyx cutter (OP R13a)

Six-petal pointed blossom sets (OP N1–N8)

Plain-edged cutting wheel (PME)

STAMENS

1 Bend a group of four stamens in half to form eight seedhead stamens. Add an extra stamen for the pistil if desired. Glue together with a little non-toxic hi-tack glue. Squeeze the glue onto the length of the stamens, flattening them as you go. Leave a short length of the group unglued from the tips. Glue the end of a 28-gauge wire onto the flattened stamens. Pinch and wrap the stamens around the wire to secure the two together. Allow to dry before dusting the tips with primrose and lemon petal dust.

PETALS

2 Roll out either some white or pale lemon flowerpaste, leaving a fine ridge. Cut out a petal shape. Insert a moistened 30-gauge white wire into the ridge. Pinch the petal at the base to secure and elongate the petal shape. Thin out the rounded end of the petal to form a slight point using a celstick.

3 Cut out fine, slender V-shaped cuts from the edges of each petal to fringe them, using either a sharp scalpel or a fine pair of scissors. Now thin out the edges with the veining tool and then vein each of the individual sections and the main body of the petal. Pinch the base and tip between finger and thumb and allow it to firm slightly in a curved position. Do not let the petals dry completely before you dust them. Repeat to make a total of two petals.

4 The tiny petals are made with floristry tape. Simply tape the ends of three 33-gauge wires with quarter-width tape, leaving a flap of tape at the end of each. Snip the sides of each flap for a feathered look. Pinch and stretch the tape for a more realistic petal shape.

COLOURING AND ASSEMBLY

5 First dust all the petals with primrose. Overdust the base of the two standard petals with a touch of lemon petal dust. The petals should still be wet to achieve a bright yellow. Paint tiny spots onto each petal with nasturtium liquid colour and the tip of a cocktail stick (toothpick).

6 Tape the two standard petals onto the stamens using quarter-width nile green floristry tape. The stamens should curl

towards the gap between the two petals. Next add the three small petals underneath the stamens.

CALYX

7 Form a ball of green paste into a teardrop, then pinch the base to form a hat shape. Thin out the base using a celstick. Cut out the calyx with the rose calyx cutter. Open up the centre with the pointed end of the celstick to represent the opening of the nectary. Soften the edges and vein the centre of each sepal using a dresden tool.

8 Moisten the calyx centre and thread it onto the back of the flower, positioning each sepal to cover joins in the petals. Insert the wire just below the nectary opening, piercing straight through the calyx underneath the nectary opening at the back. Pinch the calyx onto the flower to secure it. Curl the tip of the nectary down and lift the whole length of the nectary to a higher position on the back of the flower. Dust lightly with vine green.

BUDS

9 The buds similarly exhibit fine, curled nectaries. They look like tadpoles at first before you curl up the nectary. Wire each onto 28-gauge wires. Pinch the tip of each between two fingers and a thumb to give the bud a three-sided shape at the tip. Dust as for the calyx. Tape over each stem with green tape.

LEAVES

10 Pinch a piece of green paste to form a pimple at the centre, then roll it out

around the pimple. Cut out the leaf using one of the eight sizes of pointed blossom cutter. Cut off one of the petal shapes with the sharp scalpel.

11 Lengthen the central section with a celstick, then broaden all of the sections in turn. Turn the leaf over and

vein the centre of each section using the plain-edged cutting wheel or a dresden tool. Turn the leaf over again. Make an open hook in the end of a 24-, 26-, or 28-gauge wire, depending upon the size of the leaf. Bend the wire so that the main length of the wire comes out from the centre of this loop to form a ski-stick shape. Heat the end of the wire over a naked flame. When the wire is red hot, aim it at the pimple on the back of the leaf. The sugar will caramelize and cool quickly to form a good bond between the two. Pinch the tips of each section and allow to firm up before dusting.

12 Dust in turn with forest, vine green and then holly/ivy mixed with a little white dust. Allow to dry and then dip into a quarter glaze or steam. Etch away the veins on each section using a sharp scalpel. Tape over each of the leaf stems with nile green floristry tape.

13 Tape the components onto a single 22-gauge wire to start with, adding more wire as you need it if you are making a long stem. Note that each time you tape in a flower bud you should also tape in a leaf. Dust the stems with vine green petal dust. Bend the whole stem into the required shape.

PHRAGMIPEDIUM ORCHID

Phragmipedium is the smallest genera of the slipper orchid family. These plants are highly collectable and create much excitement among orchid collectors. I have one *Phragmipedium* that lives in my bedroom at home. The early morning sun catches the flowers from behind and lights up the plant like a flame. The flower pictured has been made using several hybrid plants as inspiration.

Materials

White and pale green flowerpaste (gum paste)

26-, 24-, 22-, 20- and 18-gauge wires

Tangerine, plum, white, primrose, lemon, vine green, holly/ivy, forest green and aubergine petal dusts

Cyclamen liquid food colour

Half glaze

Equipment

***Phragmipedium* orchid templates (see page 153) or cutters (AD)**

Sharp scalpel

Fine paintbrush

Plain-edged cutting wheel (PME)

Slipper orchid dorsal sepal veiner (GI)

Nile green floristry tape

Tweezers

SLIPPER (*LABELLUM*)

1 If you are using the templates from this book you will need to trace the design onto some card or thin plastic. Roll out some white paste not too fine. Place the slipper template from page 153 on top of the paste and cut out the paste using a sharp scalpel.

2 Soften the upper collar edges with the rounded end of a large celstick. Hollow out the centre of both sections of the slipper. Pinch and fold the two collars in towards the cupping of the petal.

3 Moisten one of the curved side edges with fresh egg white and then overlap the two edges. Use the rounded end of a large celstick to help blend the join and maintain the slipper shape. Press the paste firmly with your thumb against the stick to blend the join as best you can. Hollow out the slipper a little more if required.

4 Carefully curl in the top sections of the slipper to form a thicker part to the upper section, as this will need extra support when the wire is added. Pinch a central vein on the front of the slipper using your finger and thumb. Allow to rest for about half an hour before the next step.

5 Bend a hook in the end of a 20-gauge wire. Cover the wire with a fine layer of white paste. Soften some more paste with fresh egg white and coat one side of the padded wire with it. Bend the padded hook at an angle and pull through the top section of the slipper. Try to blend the paste as best you can onto the back section of the slipper using a dresden tool. Allow to dry overnight.

ANTHER CAP/COLUMN

6 The column and anther cap (and the stamens) are fused together in complex formation! Here is a simplified version. Form a cone shape of white paste. Flatten the broad end and then pinch one half of the flattened piece into a point. Indent the opposite section with the scalpel to form a heart shape. Moisten the top of the slipper and attach the anther cap over the top, which should hide most of the mechanics underneath.

7 Dust the anther cap and the two folded collars with a light mixture of primrose and lemon petal dust. Dust the slipper heavily with a mixture of plum and tangerine with a touch of white added. Overdust from the base with the two colours minus the white to create more depth. Using a fine paintbrush and the cyclamen liquid colour, add some fine spots onto the two collars.

LATERAL PETALS (WING PETALS)

8 Roll out a length of white paste leaving a thick ridge for wire. Cut out the petal shape using a cutter or the template from page 153. Insert a moistened 26-gauge wire into about half the length of the petal. Soften the edges and then create some fine veins from the base to the tip using the plain-edged cutting wheel. Pinch the base of the petal back on itself and pinch the tip forwards. Many of the phragmipedium orchids have twisted side petals, some have broader and flatter side petals as well. I tend to twist these petals to give the flower more interest. Repeat to make an opposite petal.

DORSAL AND BASE SEPAL

9 These are both made in the same way. Roll out some paste leaving a thick ridge. Cut out the sepal shape. Insert a moistened 26-gauge wire. Soften the edges and then vein using the double-sided slipper orchid veiner. Pinch the sepal from the base to the tip. Cup the centre of the sepal slightly. Curl back the side edges and allow to firm up over a gentle curve. Repeat the process to make the two shapes.

10 Dust the base of the petals and sepals with primrose and lemon petal dust. Add the tangerine/plum mix to a greater or lesser degree, working from the tips and then the base of each shape. The two wing petals usually have some very fine hair at the base, which I tend to represent by painting some tiny cyclamen dots at the base of each one.

11 Tape the two wing petals on either side of the slipper. Add an 18-gauge wire to lengthen and strengthen the stem. Next add the dorsal and base sepals. You will need to be very careful not to damage the long side petals, I'm sure you don't need me to tell you that!

OVARY

12 Attach a sausage of green paste to the back of the flower. Thin out either end and then pinch a series of fine lines onto the surface using a pair of tweezers. Dust with holly/ivy and vine

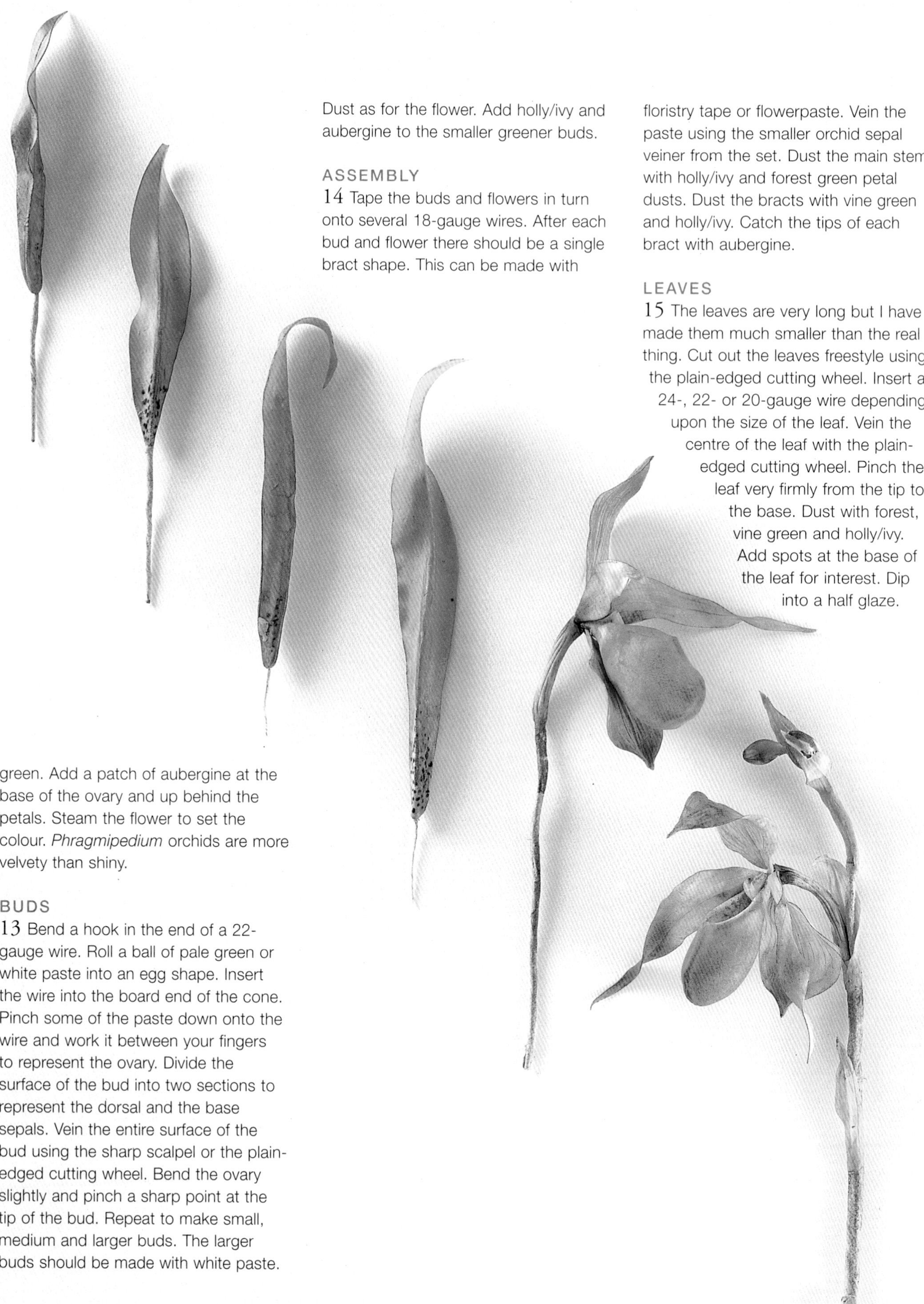

green. Add a patch of aubergine at the base of the ovary and up behind the petals. Steam the flower to set the colour. *Phragmipedium* orchids are more velvety than shiny.

BUDS

13 Bend a hook in the end of a 22-gauge wire. Roll a ball of pale green or white paste into an egg shape. Insert the wire into the board end of the cone. Pinch some of the paste down onto the wire and work it between your fingers to represent the ovary. Divide the surface of the bud into two sections to represent the dorsal and the base sepals. Vein the entire surface of the bud using the sharp scalpel or the plain-edged cutting wheel. Bend the ovary slightly and pinch a sharp point at the tip of the bud. Repeat to make small, medium and larger buds. The larger buds should be made with white paste. Dust as for the flower. Add holly/ivy and aubergine to the smaller greener buds.

ASSEMBLY

14 Tape the buds and flowers in turn onto several 18-gauge wires. After each bud and flower there should be a single bract shape. This can be made with floristry tape or flowerpaste. Vein the paste using the smaller orchid sepal veiner from the set. Dust the main stems with holly/ivy and forest green petal dusts. Dust the bracts with vine green and holly/ivy. Catch the tips of each bract with aubergine.

LEAVES

15 The leaves are very long but I have made them much smaller than the real thing. Cut out the leaves freestyle using the plain-edged cutting wheel. Insert a 24-, 22- or 20-gauge wire depending upon the size of the leaf. Vein the centre of the leaf with the plain-edged cutting wheel. Pinch the leaf very firmly from the tip to the base. Dust with forest, vine green and holly/ivy. Add spots at the base of the leaf for interest. Dip into a half glaze.

Crocosmia Berries

Crocosmia, which has wonderful orange-red flowers during the summer months, produces interesting berries in late summer and early autumn. These berries are available almost all year round from florists and help soften the edges of display work. They are very simple to make.

Materials

30-, 28-, 24- and 20-gauge wires

Pale holly/ivy flowerpaste (gum paste)

Vine, holly/ivy, aubergine, tangerine and red petal dusts

Half glaze

Equipment

Fine-nosed pliers

Sharp scalpel

Nile green floristry tape

BERRIES

1 Cut several short lengths of 30- and 28-gauge wire. Bend a hook in the end of each with the pliers. Roll a small ball of flowerpaste and insert a moistened wire into the base. The gauge will depend upon the size of the berry.

2 Divide the surface of the berry into three sections using a sharp scalpel. Pinch a ridge down the centre of each of the sections with your finger and thumb. Repeat to make lots of berries in varying sizes.

ASSEMBLY

3 Tape the berries onto a 24-gauge wire to begin with, gradually introducing a stronger gauge further down the stem.

The berries should start at the top of the stem with the smallest first, gradually working down to the larger ones. Sometimes this can work in reverse but for this purpose it looks better if the sizes gradate. Alternate the position of the berries as you add them to the stem. There should be two tiny bracts at the base of each of the berries but I have left them off. Put it down to a bit of artistic licence!

COLOURING

4 It is easier to dust these berries when they are in place. Dust to varying degrees with vine, holly/ivy, tangerine, red and aubergine. Dip into a half glaze, glazing the stem as well. You might prefer to colour and glaze the berries before you assemble the whole stem.

Coelogyne Ochracea

When the flower spikes are maturing the buds can be seen behind a fine veil of green membrane. The veil splits and the buds are released. The buds do not open gradually as do many orchids, they all open together! The flower spike is covered with wonderfully scented little orchids!

Materials

White flowerpaste (gum paste)

Vine green, holly/ivy and egg yellow petal dusts

Ruby red paste colour

Clear alcohol (kirsch or Cointreau)

30- and 20-gauge wires

Cornflour (cornstarch)

Equipment

Dendrobium orchid column mould (HH)

Dendrobium orchid lip cutter/veiner (HH)

Cutters (TT23, 458, 325)

Nile green floristry tape

PREPARATION

1 Use the column mould and white paste and make as many columns as you will need for the spray of orchids, or for the bouquet if you are going to use them as 'pipped' orchids. Hollow the underside of the lip and cut off about 0.5cm (¼in) from the back of the column.

2 Roll out white paste, dust with cornflour and cut out the lip. Clean off the cut edge and press the paste against the veining part of the cutter with your thumb. Remove from the cutter/veiner. Cut off just over 0.5cm (¼in) from the back of the veiner.

3 Frill the edge of the lip with a frilling tool. Dust the centre of the sides of the orchid, the callus and the centre of the lip with egg yellow. Turn the lip so the front edge points away from you and using the ruby paste colour moistened with clear alcohol, paint a shaky looking heart shape in the centre, with the point towards the callus. Now paint an outline inside the edge of the petal. Very carefully moisten the back and sides of the lip and attach it to the column.

4 Roll out a sausage of white paste, leaving a thickened band at one end. Cut out sepals with the TT23 cutter. Insert a hooked, moistened 30-gauge wire into the thickened paste. Soften the edges, elongate one sepal and then cup the sepals. Leave to dry. Repeat to make the lateral petals using the TT458 cutter.

5 Now make the bracts for each flower with cutter TT325, but instead of cupping them, mark a vein down the centre of each bract.

BUDS

6 Take a small piece of white paste, roll into a slender barrel shape and insert a moistened quarter-length of white 30-gauge wire into the bud. Mark with a 3-wired cage made from 30-gauge wire.

COLOURING

7 First lightly dust the sepals with vine green and then a very light touch of holly/ivy down the central vein. Dust the base of the petals and sepals with a delicate touch of vine green.

ASSEMBLY

8 Tape the lateral petals immediately to the back and side of the column and lip. Then add the lateral sepals and lastly the dorsal sepal, which is the one that was elongated. Tape the bract a little way down the stem, approximately 0.5cm (¼in).

9 Starting with the buds, tape them onto the 20-gauge wire, then add the flowers. As you go down the wire you should increase the spacing slightly between each of the flowers.

Equipment and Techniques

This section contains a list of the basic equipment and techniques required to make the sugar flowers and foliage featured in the book. Special pieces of equipment for specific cakes or flowers are listed with each set of instructions. Most of the equipment is available from specialist cake decorating suppliers.

EQUIPMENT

Board and Rolling Pin

A non-stick board and rolling pin are essential for rolling out flowerpaste. A dark green non-stick board can be preferable to a white board, which tends to strain the eyes. You may also prefer to use a grooved board to make thick central ridges on petals and leaves. These are available in the shops, but you can also make grooves yourself. To do this, heat a metal skewer until it turns red hot, then press the skewer onto the back of your non-stick board, sliding the skewer forwards. Continue heating and repeating the process until you have achieved the depth you want. The sliding movement gives a tapering groove. It is best to have grooves of different thicknesses, large, medium and small. You should leave sufficient room on either side of the groove to roll out paste for appropriate sized leaves. The large groove should be the depth of the skewer and positioned at the centre of one end of the board, to allow the full width of the board for rolling out paste. At the other end, not too close to the edge, make deep and shallow indentations with a cake testing needle for the medium and small grooves, respectively. Scrape off any excess plastic and then smooth the board with some fine glass paper.

Celsticks

Available in four sizes: small, medium, large and extra large. One end of each tool is pointed and the other is rounded. The pointed end is used to open up the centres of flowers and can also be used for veining. The rounded end is used rather like a dog bone tool, and has the advantage of a range of different sized tools for the various sizes of flowers and leaves. The central part of each of the celsticks can also be used as a rolling pin for flowers formed from a pedestal shape. They are also used for rolling thick ridges on paste, needed for wired petals and leaves.

Ceramic Silk Veining Tool & Smooth Ceramic Tool (HP)

The silk veining tool has veins on the surface; when rolled over the paste it gives a delicate texture. It can also frill the edges of petals, veining them at the same time. The smooth ceramic tool is similar in shape to the veining tool but has no markings on it. It is very useful for curling rose petals.

Cutters

There are many different types of cutters available. Cutters speed up the flower-making process and lend consistency and accuracy to your work. Metal cutters come in a greater variety of shapes and can be adjusted by bending. Plastic cutters are ideal for the intricate working involved in foliage. Most cutters used in this book are readily available from good cake decorating shops, though some will need to be ordered.

Dresden/Veining Tool

The black dresden/veining tool made by Jem is particularly good. The fine end is used for drawing veins down the centre of petals, sepals and leaves. The broad end is used to draw veins and to hollow out the edges and centres of petals and leaves. It can also be used to create an effect known as 'double frilling'. This gives a 'serrated look' and is ideal for creating jagged or ragged edges to leaves and petals.

Floristry Tape

Paper floristry tape is available in many colours, but the most commonly used are nile green, dark green, white, beige, twig and brown. The tape has a glue in it that is released when the paper is stretched, so it is important to stretch the tape firmly as you tape over a wire.

Florists' Staysoft

This is a form of plasticine, sold by florists' suppliers and some cake-decorating shops and art shops in long blocks. Arranging flowers in staysoft allows them to be removed and re-arranged if necessary. A container or disc must be used so that it does not come into contact with the cake.

Foam Pads

These are used to hold paste while you soften or vein a petal or leaf. There are several commercially available pads. If you are buying a pad for the first time, it must be firm and have a fine texture.

Great Impressions (GI) Veiners

These are double-sided rubber veiners moulded from real flowers and foliage. They add realism to flower work. Once you have cut out the leaf or petal and inserted a wire, place the shape into the veiner (the ridge on the paste should fit into the back piece of the veiner). Press the two sides together firmly and then remove the leaf, now veined on both sides to a natural finish. You will need to assess the thickness of paste required for some of the more heavily veined petals and leaves – if you make the paste too fine the veiner may cut through it!

Lace Cutters

There are several makes now available. They are ideal for people who have difficulty piping lace. A mixture of sugarpaste and Mexican paste or flowerpaste is best to use with these cutters. A sharp, angled palette knife is ideal for cutting away excess paste. Always smooth the lace in the cutter with a smidgen of fat on the finger to remove any rough edges. These lace pieces may be set over different shapes to curve them attractively before fixing them to the cake.

Leather Punches

These are usually made from stainless steel but may also be made from toughened plastic. They act as both a cutter and a veiner and produce small, sharp cut-outs. They may be obtained from many leather workshops, in particular there are several branches of Tandy Leather both in the United Kingdom and America. One branch is situated in 5th Avenue very near the Empire State Building.

Metal Ball Tools

Metal ball tools are intended for use with Cold Porcelain, but they work equally well on sugar. More comfortable than plastic dog bone tools, they can be used in exactly the same way but create beautifully flowing fluting at the edge of the petal if rolled along the edge.

Metal Frilling Sticks

Used to soften the edges of petals, these tools create a completely different look than that achieved with a dog bone or with a ball tool. A cocktail or saté stick (toothpick) can also be used, but the metal tool is kinder to the fingers.

Non-toxic Hi-tack Glue (Impex)

This is a non-toxic glue used to glue stamens onto wire. It is safe to use on flowers with wires in them but should not come into immediate contact with cake surfaces. Note that this type of glue is not permissible for use on competition work.

Handel's Messiah rose, page 130

Non-toxic Glue Stick

This is a basic glue stick available in most stationery shops and is used for fixing ribbons to cake boards.

Paintbrushes

Good brushes are one of the most important items in a flower-maker's kit. Remember that the final control and accuracy with colouring can make or break your work. Flat brushes are the most useful for dusting flowers and foliage (round brushes are not firm enough to colour accurately with dusting powders). Brushes by Robert Simmons called Craft Painters nos. 6 and 8 are particularly recommended, along with their Shaders. You will need a good selection of finer brushes for painting fine details on flowers and foliage. We find that it is preferable to use a different brush for each main colour to avoid the problem of dirty colouring

Plain-edged Cutting Wheel (P.M.E.)

A 'must have' for any sugarcrafter's workbox, this tool enables you to cut pastillage or flowerpaste without any 'pulling' and gives very good control when cutting out leaves and petals freehand. There is a large and a small wheel at either end of the tool.

Pliers and Wire Cutters

Small, fine-nosed pliers are essential, but a good pair can be costly. They can be purchased from specialist electrical supply shops, or can be found in the jewellery sections of craft shops. Wire cutters are also very useful; either electrical cutters or a pair of heavy duty florists' scissors.

Silicone Plastique

A moulding material that can be used to create wonderful leaf veiners or moulds. It is food grade and therefore permitted for use with sugarcraft. See pages 34–5 for how to use Silicone Plastique.

Stamens

There is a vast range of stamens available to the flower-maker. You may prefer to use mainly white stamens and colour them the required colour with petal dust. Always keep a supply of small white seedhead stamens and some finer white stamens, as well as both large and small lily stamens.

Tape Shredder

This is used to cut lengths of floristry tape into various widths. If you remove one of the blades, you will have a shredder that will cut one half- and two quarter-width lengths at the same time. The blades are actually razor blades and will need to be replaced occasionally and cleaned regularly.

Textured Rolling Pins (HP)

These come in two sizes and at the time of writing in two textures: Watered

Taffeta and Dupion Silk. They have many applications; texture on the surface of a cake, on a board, on bows, for patchwork etc.

Thread

Fine, white lace-making cotton thread (Brock 120) is best used for stamens, although some thicker cotton threads can also be useful.

Wires

The quality of the wires available varies; the best wire available for sugarcrafters is Sunrise wire. If this cannot be obtained then it is best to buy A-grade wire, which can be identified by a red spot on the packet. You may prefer to buy white wire in gauges from 33-gauge (fine) to 24-gauge (thicker) and then tape over the wire with nile green floristry tape during the assembly of the flower. There are also stronger wires available from 22-gauge to 14-gauge (the higher the number, the finer the wire). These can be covered or uncovered and it doesn't matter which you use. You can also buy very fine silk-covered 36-gauge wire on a reel, which is ideal for very small flowers.

TECHNIQUES

Wiring Leaves and Petals

Roll out some flowerpaste to the required thickness, leaving a thick ridge down the centre – this can be achieved either by rolling a piece of well-kneaded paste with a large celstick, leaving the centre thicker, or by rolling out the paste on a grooved board. Cut out the petal or leaf shape using a cutter or template. You will need to position the cutter so that the ridge of paste runs from the tip to the base of the leaf or petal. Press the cutter down firmly, then release the paste from the cutter. (You may find that you end up with cleaner cut edges if you scrub the cutter and paste against the board.) Moisten the end of a wire and insert it into the thick ridge, holding the paste firmly between your finger and thumb to prevent the end of the wire from piercing through. You should always insert the wire into at least half the length of the paste ridge. This will ensure that the petal or leaf gets adequate support and is not likely to bend under its own weight.

Dog's-tooth violets, pages 94–95

Colouring

A limited selection of paste or liquid food colourings is required. Dusting powders (petal dust) may also be used to colour the paste, but are usually used for colouring after shaping. If you decide to mix powders into flowerpaste as colouring, avoid large amounts as they can alter the consistency. You may find it preferable to colour the paste a paler shade of the colour you want the finished flower to be, then dust on top to achieve greater depth. It is important to have a good selection of dusting powder colours and to experiment with different colour combinations to obtain the effect you want. The colours can either be mixed together or simply brushed onto the paste in layers. The instructions for each of the flowers in this book include a list of colours used. It is better to mix up a large pot of colour in advance, rather than mixing up small amounts at a time, as this wastes both time and dusting powder! If you want to make a colour paler, it will need to be mixed with white dusting powder. Sometimes a little cornflour (cornstarch) is added, but this is usually to clean the colour out of a brush and to give a very subtle tinge to the petal tips. You may need to use a few liquid colours, the main one being cyclamen, to paint detail spots and lines onto petals.

Glazing

There are several ways to add a glaze to flowers and leaves. The steaming method is used not to give a high gloss, but rather to create a 'waxy' finish or, more often, to remove the dry dusted appearance left by dusing powder. It is also used when trying to create a velvety finish or for darkening the depth of colour on a flower or a leaf, since the surface of the paste is still slightly damp after steaming. Hold each flower or leaf in the steam from a boiling kettle for a few seconds, or until the surface turns shiny. Take great care as too much steam can soften the sugar and cause it to dissolve.

For a more permanent and shiny glaze, use confectioners' varnish. Used neat (full glaze), this gives a high gloss ideal for berries and glossy leaves. For most foliage this looks too artificial, so it is better to dilute the varnish with isopropyl alcohol (available from chemists). Mix the varnish and alcohol in a lidded container and shake to mix – not too much as this will create tiny air bubbles. The glaze can be used straight away; simply dip the leaf, petal or a group of pieces into the glaze, shake off the excess and dry on absorbent kitchen paper. The glaze may be applied with a paintbrush, but the brush strokes tend to remove the colour in streaks. The following glazes are those most often used:

Three-quarters glaze

Quarter part alcohol to three-quarters varnish. This gives a semi-gloss without the 'plastic' appearance of a full glaze.

Half glaze

Equal proportions of alcohol and varnish. This gives a natural shine that is ideal for many foliages, including ivy and rose leaves.

Pompom, page 52

Quarter glaze

Three-quarters alcohol to a quarter part varnish. This is used for leaves that don't have much shine; the glaze just takes away the flat, dusty look of a leaf or petal.

Using a 'Cage'

A wire 'cage' is used to mark the impression of unopened petals on a bud. The 'cage' is made from wire, the gauge depending on the size of the bud. If you are making the bud of a five-petalled flower, you will need five pieces of wire for the 'cage'. Tape the pieces of wire together at one end with half width floristry tape and open up the cage, trying not to cross the wires at the base. Insert the modelled bud, tip or base first, depending on the effect required. Close the wires on to its surface, keeping them as evenly spaced as possible. For some buds, a more realistic effect is achieved if the paste between the wires is pinched out and thinned with your finger and thumb to form a ridge that gives the appearance of larger petals. After removing from the 'cage', twist to give a spiral effect.

Flowerpaste

The type of flowerpaste (gum paste) you use is a matter of personal preference. A paste that stretches well and does not dry out on the surface too quickly, will allow you to wire petals together whilst they are still damp (a factor that most pastes fail in). Ready-made flowerpaste (by mail order) tends to be more consistent than homemade paste, and will save you a lot of time and trouble. Make your own from the following recipe if you wish.

25ml (5 teaspoons) cold water
10ml (2 teaspoons) powdered gelatine
500g (1lb/3 cups) icing (confectioners') sugar, sifted
15ml (3 teaspoons) gum tragacanth
10ml (2 teaspoons) liquid glucose
15ml (3 teaspoons) white vegetable fat (shortening)
1 medium egg white

1 Mix the water and gelatine together in a small heatproof bowl and leave to stand for 30 minutes. Sift the icing sugar and gum tragacanth into the bowl of a heavy-duty mixer and mix.

2 Place the bowl with the gelatine mixture over a saucepan of hot water and stir until the gelatine has dissolved. Warm a teaspoon in hot water, then measure out the liquid glucose (the heat should help to ease the glucose off the spoon).

3 Add the glucose and white fat to the gelatine mixture, and continue to heat until all of the ingredients have melted and are thoroughly mixed together. Add the dissolved gelatine mixture to the icing sugar, along with the egg white. Fit the beater to the machine and turn it on at its lowest speed. Beat until mixed, then increase the speed to maximum until the paste becomes white and stringy.

4 Remove the flowerpaste from the bowl and rub a thin layer of white fat over it to prevent the outer part from drying out. Place in a plastic bag and store in an airtight container. Make sure you allow the flowerpaste to rest and to mature for at least 12 hours before using it.

Working with flowerpaste

You will need a pot of fresh egg white, a pot of cornflour (cornstarch) and white vegetable fat. The continued use of fresh egg white is far superior to any other substitutes. However, if you are doubtful about using egg white you may choose to use edible glue instead.

The paste should be kneaded well before it is modelled into a flower or rolled out on a board, otherwise it has a tendency to dry out and crack around the edges. If the paste is dry or tough, then soften it using fresh egg white (not gum arabic etc) – do not add it in large quantities as this will make the paste short, difficult to work with and it will take longer to dry.

If the paste is sticky, then a small amount of white fat may be used on the fingers while you knead it – but do not add too much! For many people, there is a temptation to add cornflour to the paste when it is sticky. However, while cornflour can be used on the surface of the paste quite happily, if it is added to flowerpaste it seems to aggravate the stickiness.

Always grease the board with white fat, then remove almost completely with absorbent kitchen paper. This will form a very thin layer of fat on the board and stop the paste gripping to the board. If you use too much fat it will show up on the finished petal or leaf when you apply dusting powder.

Although commercial paste does not tend to dry out very quickly, it is advisable if you are cutting out a large number of petals to cover them with a celflap or a plastic bag to stop the surface crusting over.

Royal Icing (with dried albumen)

This royal icing recipe is suitable for coating, piping a snail trail, as well as for shells, runouts and brush embroidery etc. The recipe will make about 2kg (4lb) of icing.

45g (3 tablespoons)
pure dried albumen powder
315ml (10fl oz/1¼ cups) water

1.75kg (3¼lb/10½ cups) icing
(confectioners') sugar, sifted

1 Wash the mixer bowl, a small bowl and the beater with a concentrated detergent and scald to remove any grease and leftover detergent.

2 Reconstitute the dried albumen with the water in a small bowl. It will become very lumpy but continue to stir and then leave it to dissolve for about 20 minutes. Then strain it into the mixer bowl.

3 Add the sifted icing sugar gradually into the albumen. Fix the bowl and beater to the electric mixer and beat on the slowest speed for 4 minutes (soft peak) or 5 minutes (full peak).

Royal Icing (with fresh egg white)

This recipe is intended for fine lace and long extension work, although it is also suitable for embroidery, snail trail and shells, omitting the tartaric and acetic acids (which are added to the egg white to alter the pH balance).

1 medium egg white
Pinch of tartaric acid
(for fine lace work)
or 2 drops of acetic acid (for long
dropped lines of extension work)
225g (8oz/1¾ cups) icing
(confectioners') sugar, sifted

1 Wash and scald the bowl and beater as described before. Place the egg white into the bowl with the pinch of tartaric acid. Add the majority of the icing sugar and mix the two together.

2 Fix the bowl to the machine and beat on the slowest speed until it has reached full peak – about 8 minutes. You may need to mix in some more sugar if the mixture is too soft.

Coating with Sugarpaste

1 Knead the sugarpaste (cold rolled fondant) to make it smooth; try not to knead too many air bubbles into it. Lightly dust the work surface with icing (confectioners') sugar. Roll out the sugarpaste to an even thickness, about 1cm (½in). Moisten the surface of the almond paste (marzipan) with clear alcohol (kirsch or Cointreau). Form an even coating of alcohol – if you have dry areas, these will be prone to forming air bubbles with the sugarpaste.

2 Lift the sugarpaste over the cake and ease it into position, smoothing out the top. Trim the sugarpaste from around the base of the cake. Polish the top and the sides using sugarpaste smoothers. You can also use a pad of sugarpaste pressed into the palm of my hand to smooth the edges and corners of the cake. If you catch the paste and make an indent, try smoothing it over with the pad of paste.

Cold Porcelain

Making cold porcelain is simple and effective, but you will be dealing with chemicals and must consider safety factors. If you have asthma or any other chest complaint we would suggest that you use a commercial paste and follow the instructions on the packet. Work in a well ventilated room and wear a mask as the paste gives off fumes during the cooking process.

To make the paste we use two specific glues. The combination is that of a non-toxic hi-tack glue (which provides elasticity) and a wood glue (for strength). If you live abroad or in areas where they are not available you will have to do what we did, experiment until you find a combination you like. In all cases the proportion of glue to cornflour is usually equal. Some glues require the addition of a little more cornflour. The quantity of oil used depends on how soft you like your paste to feel. For added softness add a little more oil.

Homemade cold porcelain must never be placed in contact with a food product and must not be used as an alternative to flowerpaste for cake decoration. We recommend its use for non-edible items such as floral arrangements, plants in candleholders, corsages, bouquets, etc.

2–3 tablespoons baby oil
125ml (4fl oz/½ cup) non-toxic
hi-tack glue (Impex)
125ml (4fl oz/½ cup) super
woodglue (Liberon)
1 cup cornflour (cornstarch)

1 Measure the oil into a medium-sized non-stick pan and add the glue. Stir them together to a thick cream. Add 1 cup of cornflour and stir it in. Place over medium heat until the paste has collected around the spoon as for choux pastry. Scrape any uncooked paste from the spoon as you are cooking. The paste should feel spongy to the touch.

2 Turn the paste onto a non-stick board. Cover with clingfilm and allow to cool for a few minutes. Like bread dough the paste will cling to your fingers at the beginning. Resist adding extra cornflour unless there is no sign that it is coming off your fingers. Do not add more than the extra ¼ cup as it is very difficult to soften the paste again. It is better to have a softer paste which will stiffen as you work it in your hands.

4 Wrap the paste in clingfilm, place it in a plastic bag and store in an air-tight container. Do not place in a refrigerator as the cold will break down the glue!

Cold porcelain will dry slightly yellow and translucent unless permanent white gouache is kneaded into the paste. Colour added to the paste changes its consistency, so it is better to add it just before use. Remember that as the cold porcelain shrinks as it dries any colour added to the paste will deepen. As a rough guide to how much white gouache should be added, try the following: Circle the middle finger and thumb of your right hand. Take a piece of paste and roll it into a ball about the size of the circle. Flatten the paste. Now squeeze out permanent white gouache from a tube about the length of the top joint of the little finger of that same hand (disregarding the nail!) and knead it into the paste.

TEMPLATES

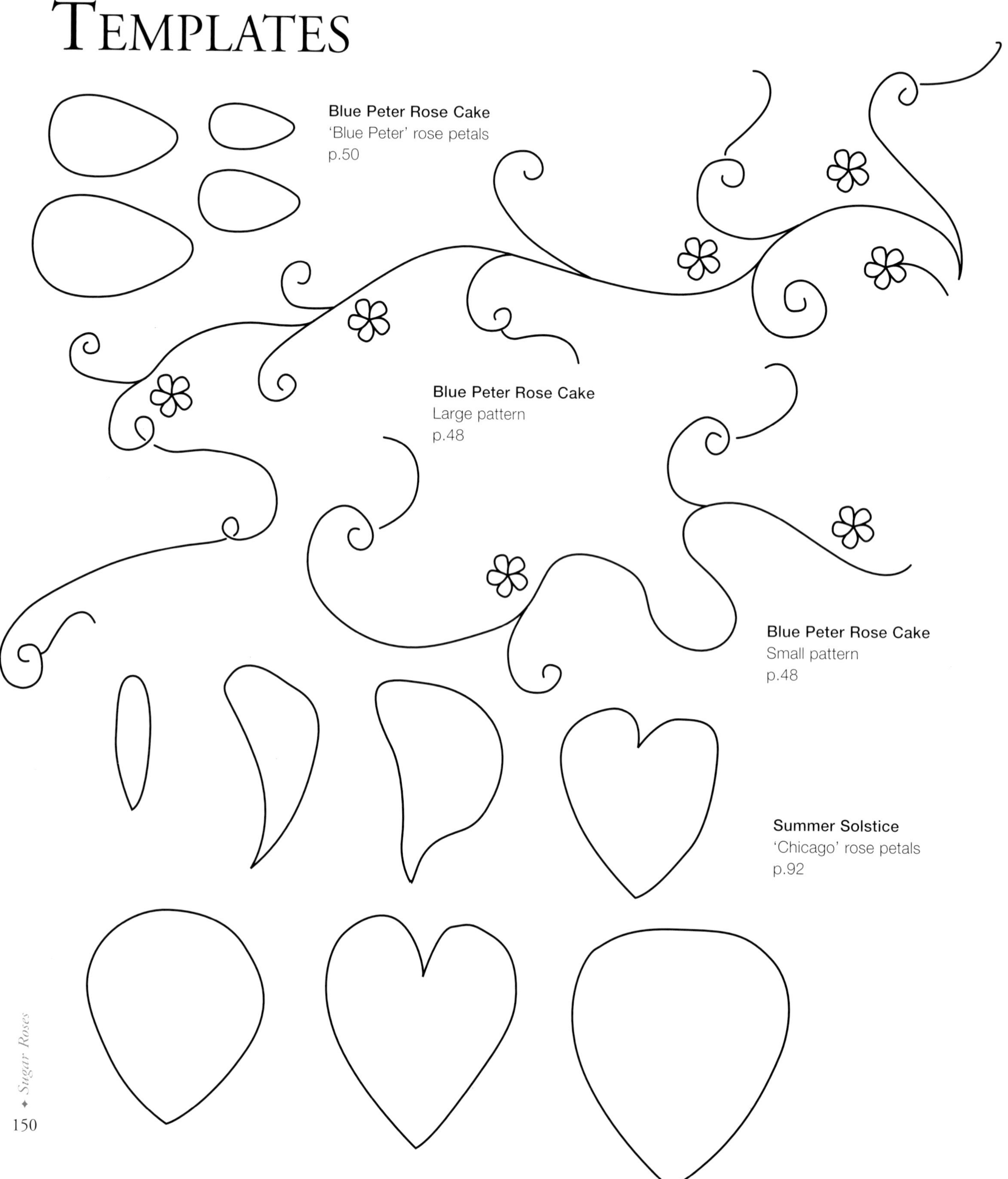

Blue Peter Rose Cake
'Blue Peter' rose petals
p.50
Blue Peter Rose Cake
Large pattern
p.48
Blue Peter Rose Cake
Small pattern
p.48
Summer Solstice
'Chicago' rose petals
p.92

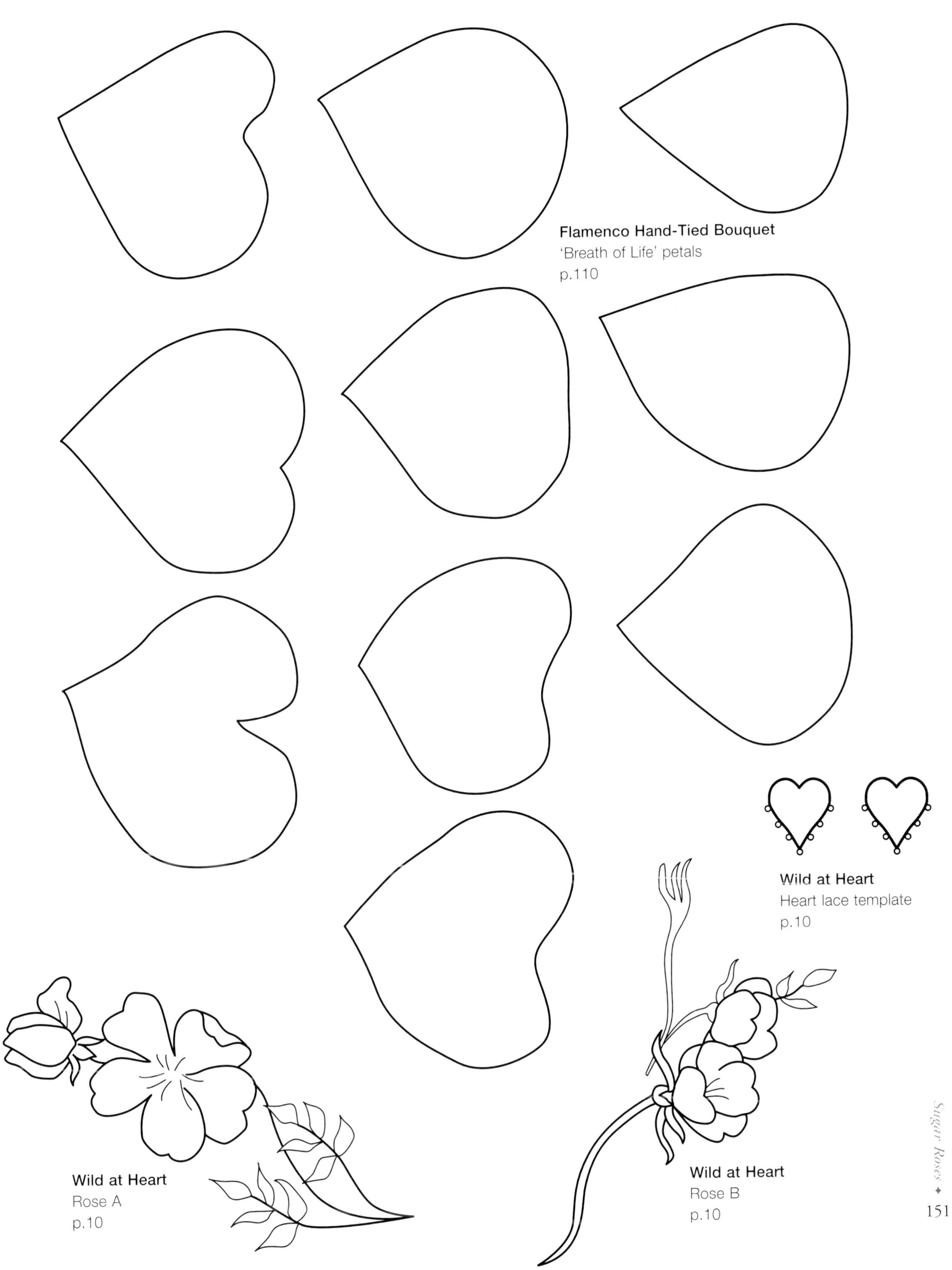

Flamenco Hand-Tied Bouquet
'Breath of Life' petals
p.110

Wild at Heart
Heart lace template
p.10

Wild at Heart
Rose A
p.10

Wild at Heart
Rose B
p.10

side single
A
D
Diamond Jubilee
Frame
p.70
photocopy at 200%
top design
B
C
side pair
lace
'Diamond Jubilee' rose
petals
p.74

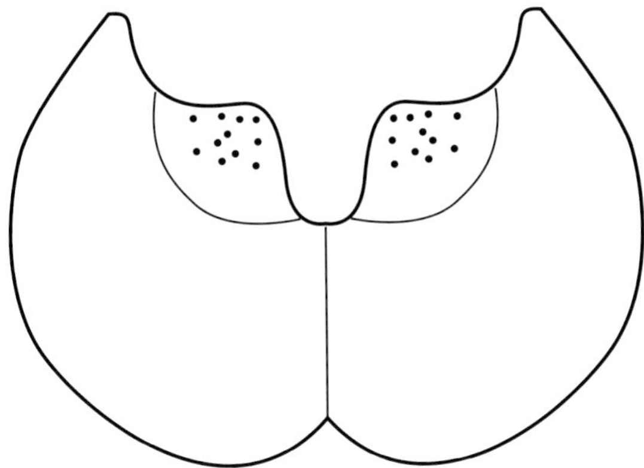

White Rose and Orchid Bridal Bouquet
Phragmipedium orchid slipper
pp.140-141

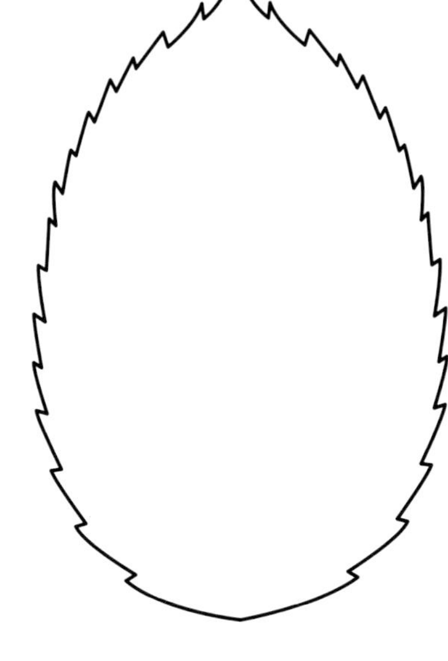

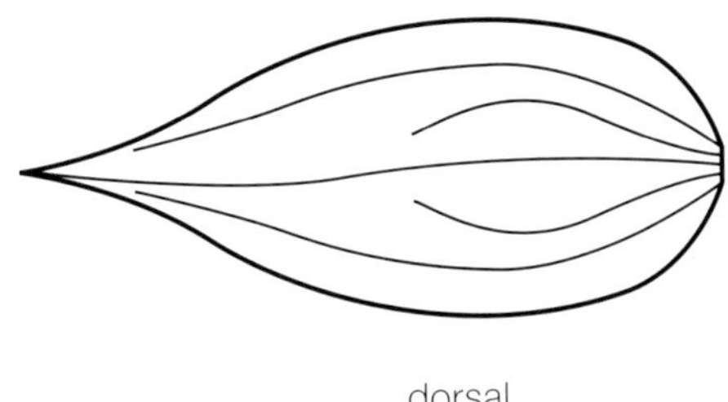

dorsal

'Painter' rose
leaves
p.80

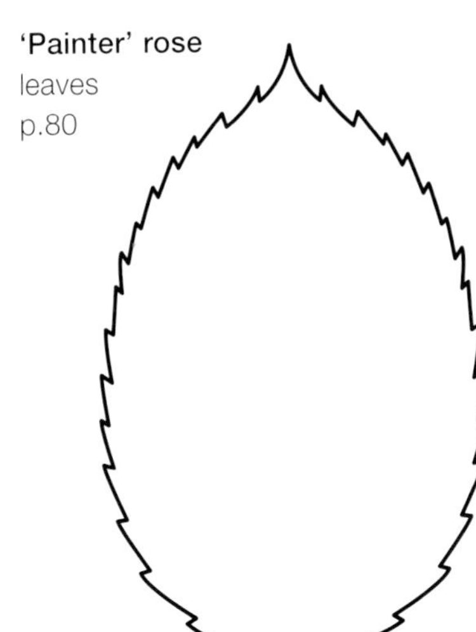

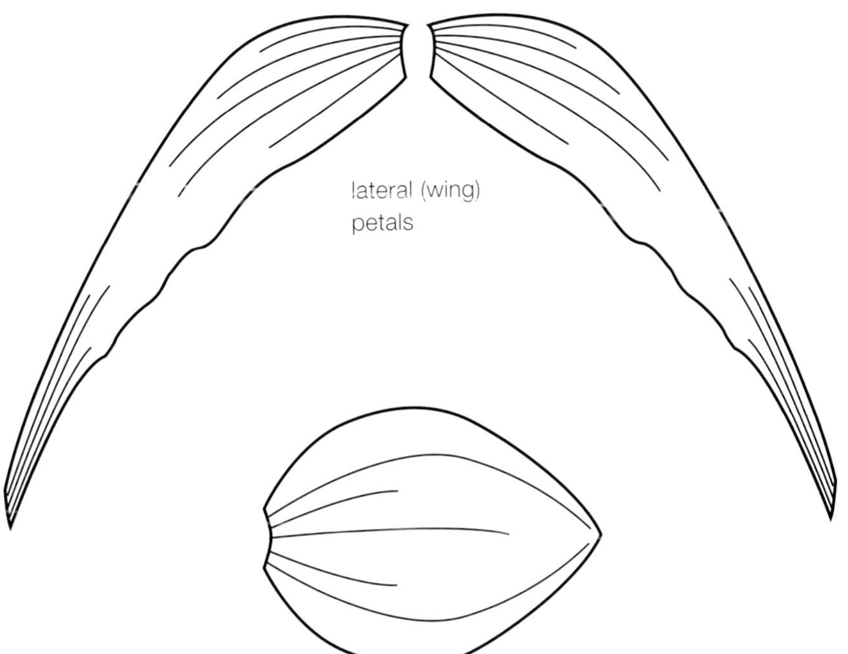

lateral (wing)
petals

base

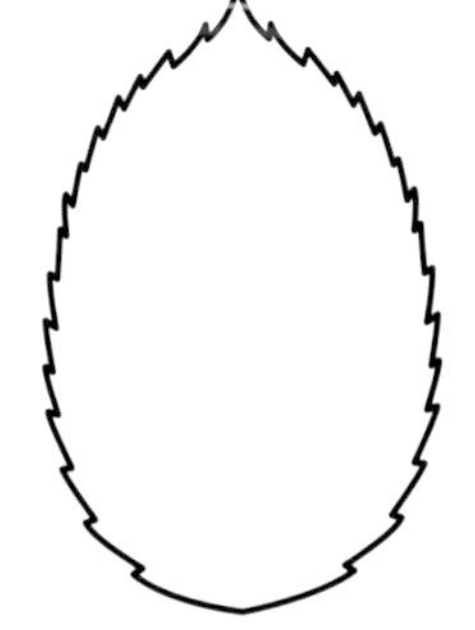

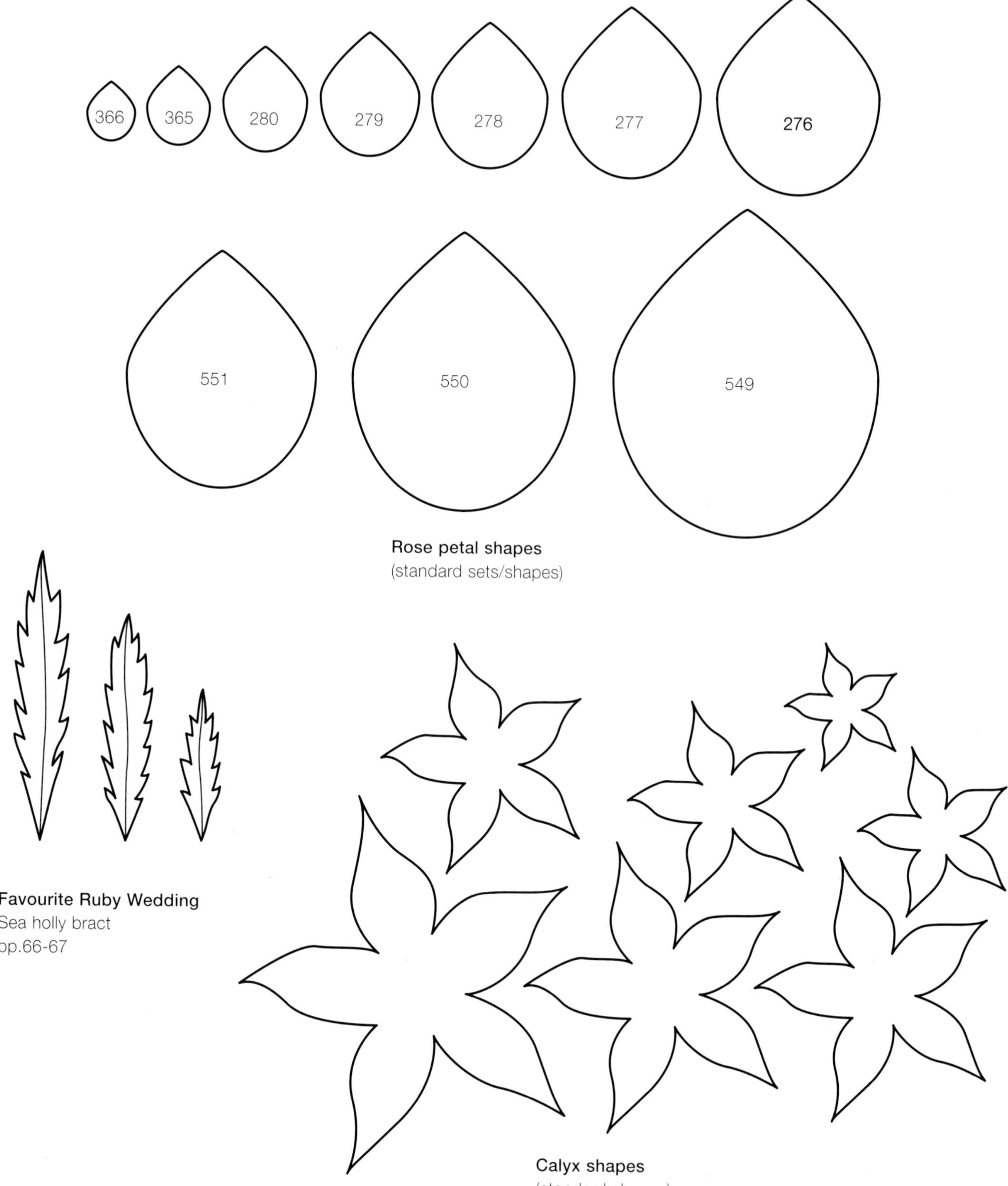

Rose petal shapes
(standard sets/shapes)

Favourite Ruby Wedding
Sea holly bract
pp.66-67

Calyx shapes
(standard shapes)

Quilted Box Cake
p.100

Susan's Wedding Cake
Arum lily, spadix and spathe
p.89

Starfish and Coral
Beetleweed leaf
p.121

Starfish and Coral
'Quick' rose blossom shape
p.118

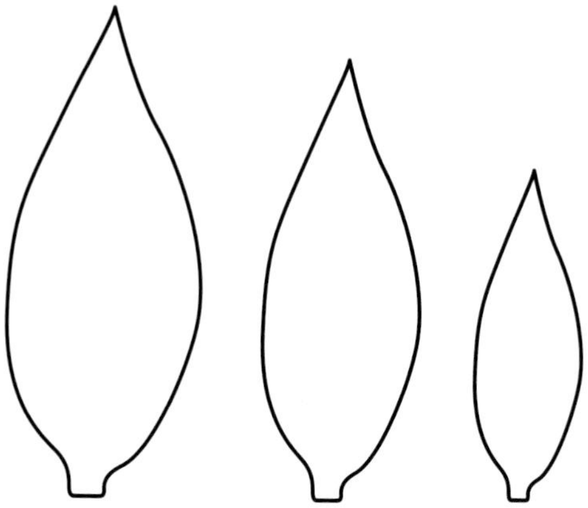

Susan's Wedding Cake
Tradescantia
p.88

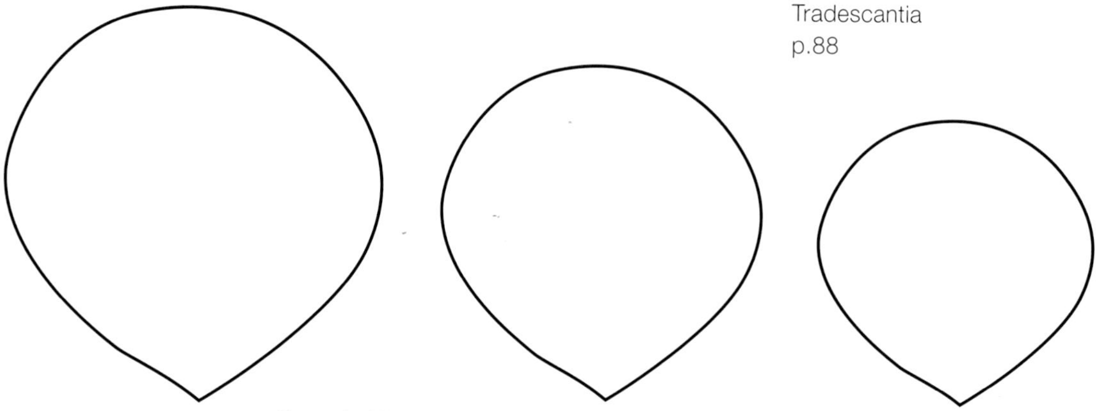

Susan's Wedding Cake
'Delilah' petals
p.86

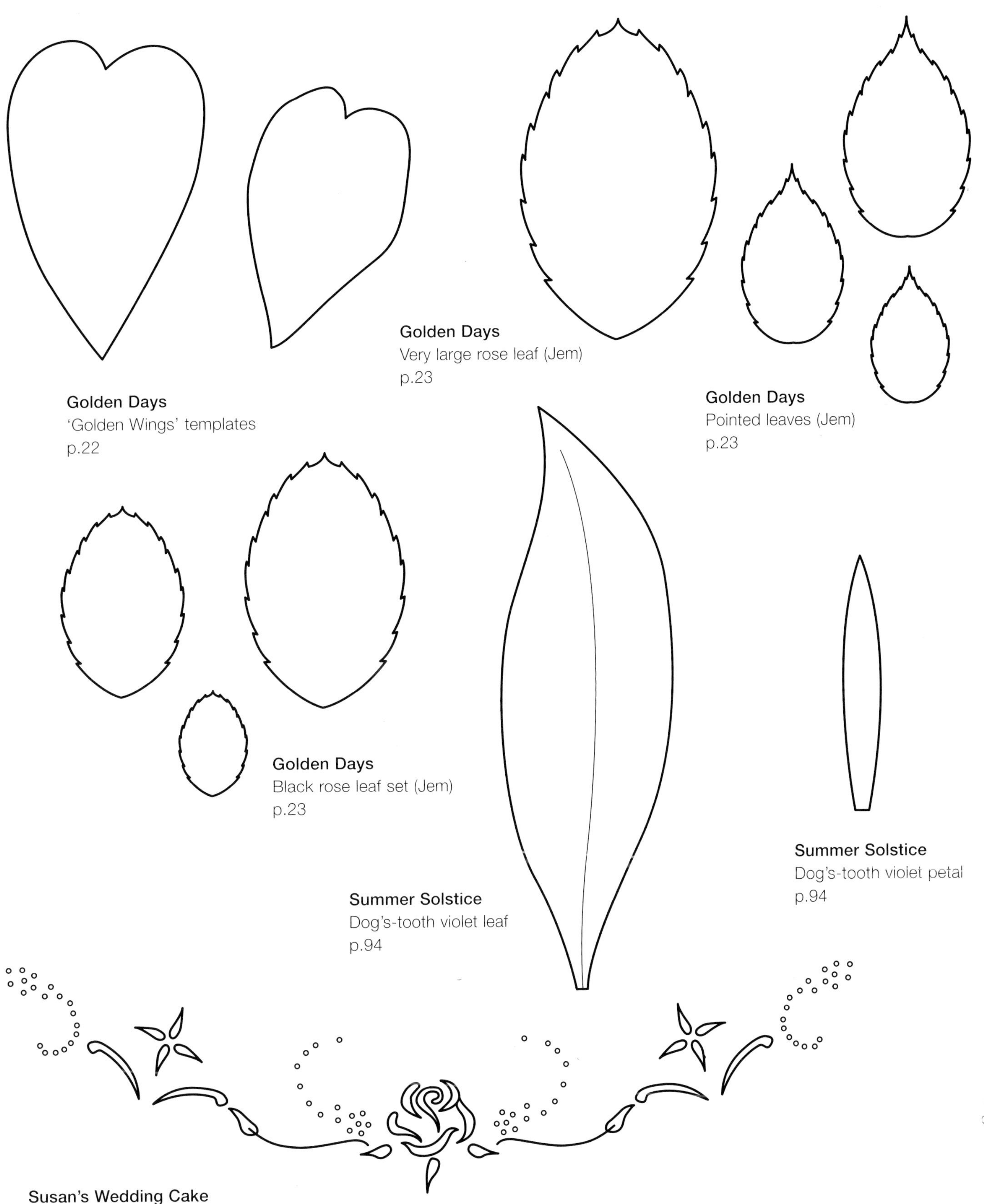

Golden Days
'Golden Wings' templates
p.22

Golden Days
Very large rose leaf (Jem)
p.23

Golden Days
Pointed leaves (Jem)
p.23

Golden Days
Black rose leaf set (Jem)
p.23

Summer Solstice
Dog's-tooth violet leaf
p.94

Summer Solstice
Dog's-tooth violet petal
p.94

Susan's Wedding Cake
Embroidery pattern
p.84

INDEX

A
A Basket of Roses 106–7
arrangements
Contemporary Arrangements 122–3
Driftwood Arrangement 72–3
White Christmas 26–35
Winter Wedding 124–9
appleberries, purple 19
arum lily 89

B
bear grass 121
beetleweed 121
berries
Crocosmia 143
mahonia 68
Billardiera longiflora 19
bittersweet, Oriental climbing 128–9
blood lilies 114–15
Blue Peter Rose Cake 48–51
'Blue Peter' rose 50–51
'Boule de neige' rose 28–30
bouquets
White Rose and Orchid Bridal Bouquet 136–144
Flamenco Hand-Tied Bouquet 108–15
Hand-Tied Bouquet 129
'Breath of Life' rose 110–12

C
cakes
Blue Peter Rose Cake 48–51
Danish Romance 36–40
Diamond Jubilee 70–7
Favourite Ruby Wedding 62–9
Golden Days 20–5
Medieval Harvest Medley 16–19
Pero's Pearl Cake 98–9
Pink Perfection 44–7
Pompom Cake, The 52–9
Quilted Box Cake 100–6
Starfish and Coral 116–21
Summer Solstice 90–6
Susan's Wedding Cake 84–9
Wild at Heart 10–15
'Canary creeper' 138–9
'Cathedral Splendour' rose 57–9
Celastrus 128–9
'Chicago' rose 92–3
Coelogyne ochracea 144
Contemporary Arrangements 122–3
corsages 97
Crocosmia berries 143

D
Danish Romance 36–40
'Delilah' rose 86–7
Diamond Jubilee 70–7
'Diamond Jubilee' rose displays
A Basket of Roses 106–7
'Painter' Rose Displays 78–83
Dog rose 12–15
dog's-tooth violet 94–5
Driftwood arrangement 72–3

E
'Elegance' rose 104–6
equipment 145–7
Eryngium 66–7
Erythronium 94–5
eucalyptus leaves 69

F
Favourite Ruby Wedding 62–9
Flamenco Hand-Tied Bouquet 108–15
flowerpaste 148

G
Galax viceolata 121
ginger, white 135
glazing 147–8
Golden Days 20–5
'Golden Wings' rose 22–5
gymea lilies 132–3

H
Haemanthus katherinae 114–15
Hand-Tied Bouquet 129
Handel's Messiah 130–5
hips, *Rosa rugosa* 18

I
ivy 77

L
leaves
bear grass 121
beetleweed 121
dog's-tooth violet 94–5
eucalyptus leaves 69
ivy 77
ruscus 96
tradescantia 88
vine leaves 113
white poplar 30
lilies
arum lilies 89
blood lilies 114–15
gymea lilies 132–3

M
'Mme. Cécile Brünner' rose 46–7
mahonia berries 68
'Massai' rose 126–7
Medieval Harvest Medley 16–19
Miltonia flavescens 32–3

O
'Old Blush' rose 54–5
orchids
Coelogyne ochracea 144
Miltonia flavescens 32–3
phragmipedium orchid 140–2
Oriental climbing bittersweet 128–9

P
'Painter' Rose Displays 78–83
'Pascali' rose 103
'Peppermint' rose 118–20
Pero's Pearl Cake 98–9
Phragmipedium orchid 140–2
'Pink Favourite' rose 64–5
Pink Perfection 44–7
Pompom Cake, The 52–9
poplar, white 30
purple appleberries 19

Q
'Queen of Denmark' rose 38–40
'quick' rose 118–20
Quilted Box Cake 100–6

R
roses
'Blue Peter' 48–51
'Boule de neige' 28–30
'Breath of Life' 110–12
'Cathedral Splendour' 57–9
'Chicago' 92–3
'Delilah' 86–7
'Diamond Jubilee' 74–6
dog rose 12–15
'Elegance' 104–6
'Golden Wings' 22–5
'Mme. Cécile Brünner' 46–7
'Massai' 126–7
'Old Blush' rose 54–5
'Painter' 78–83
'Pascali' 103
'Peppermint' 118–20
'Pink Favourite' 64–5
'Queen of Denmark' 38–40
'quick' rose 118–20, 122–3
Rosa rugosa hips 18
royal icing 149
ruscus 96

S
sea holly 66–7
snowberries 34–5
sprays
Handel's Messiah 130–5
Little Mermaid Spray 140–1
stamens 146
Starfish and Coral 116–21
sugarpaste 149
Summer Solstice 90–6
Susan's Wedding Cake 84–9
Symphoricarpos racemosus 34–5

T
techniques 147–9
templates 150–157
tradescantia 88
Tropaeolum canariense 138–9

V
veining tools 145, 146
violet, dog's-tooth 94–5

W
White Christmas 26–35
white ginger 135
white poplar 30
White Rose and Orchid Bridal Bouquet 136–44
white watsonia 134
Wild at Heart 10–15
Winter Wedding 124–9

X, Z
Xerophyllum tenax 121
Zantedeschia aethiopica 89

ACKNOWLEDGEMENTS

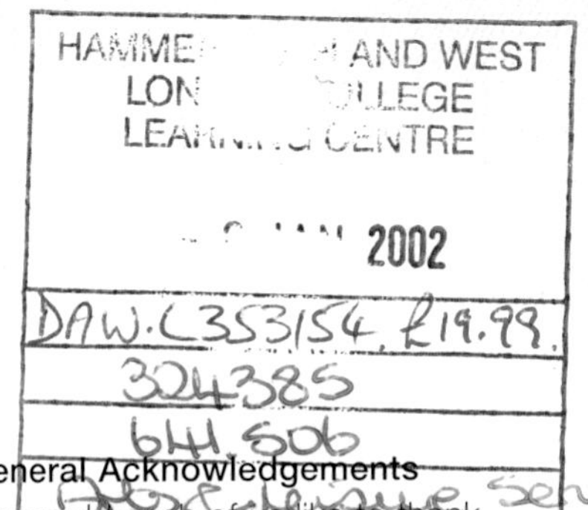

TOMBI

To Kit, Alasdair, Pero, Callum and baby Grace Victoria, with love from Grandma.

Acknowledgements

Thank you to Gladiola Botha who started it all.

TONY

To my wife Alma, daughter Emily and son Matthew with all my love.

Acknowledgements

Without the help and support of an understanding boss I would never have been able to write this book, so a very big thanks to Keith, his wife Karen, son Ben and Keith's Mum and Dad, Margaret and Geoff Clements of Confectionery Supplies. Thank you to my sisters and brothers-in-law Barbara and John, Gladys and Chris and Pam and Bill for being on the end of the phone when I needed them. Thank you to my friends Mavis and Hayward Morris, Kim and Angus Macleod and Diane and Michael Harfield for all their support over the years. And finally a big thank you to my wife Alma: without her help I would never have finished.

ALAN

I would like to dedicate this book to the memories of my Grandfather Ernest Blair, and of my friend Peter Stott.

Acknowledgements

A huge thank you to my parents Allen and Avril for their never-ending love and support. To Susan and Mark Laird for allowing me to use their wedding cake in this book! To my long-suffering friend Alice Christie who managed to keep both me and herself sane during the production of this book! Thank you also to my friends Maria Harrison, Viv Soulsby, Conor Day, Sue Burnham, Neil Parvin, Dave Meiling and Gill Pattison for all their help and support too! To Nicola and the staff at The Secret Garden for being a constant source of inspiration! A final thank you to Margaret Morland, who was the first person to teach me how to make sugar roses!

General Acknowledgements

We would each of us like to thank Renshaw Scott for supplying all the Regalice sugarpaste used in this book. Norma Laver and Jenny Walker at A Piece of Cake for the wonderful flowerpaste. June Twelves at Holly Products for the endless supply of silk veining tools. Joan Mooney at Great Impressions for supplying most of the rubber veiners. Billy and Sandra Robertson for the supply of blue pads. David and Margaret Ford for supplying a lot of the celproducts used in this book. Beverley Dutton at Squires Kitchen for the large pots of petal dust. Cornish Cake Boards for supplying the cake boards. Confectionery Supplies for their Impex glue and Silicone Plastique, and Tinker Tech 2 and Jem lines.

Thanks also to our Commissioning Editor, Barbara Croxford, for all her help and guidance, to Sue Atkinson for her superb photography, to Cathy Layzell for her design work and to Alastair Laing for his editing.

SUPPLIERS

A Piece of Cake [APOC]
18 Upper High Street
Thame, Oxon, OX9 3EX
tel./fax. 0184 421 3428
sales@apieceofcakethame.co.uk

AP Cutters [AP]
Treelands, Hillside Road
Bleadon, Weston-super-Mare
B24 OAA
tel. 01934 812 787

Cakes, Classes and Cutters
23 Princes Road
Brunton Park, Gosforth
Newcastle-upon-Tyne
NE3 5TT
tel./fax. 0191 217 0538

Celcakes and Celcrafts [C]
Springfield House
Gate Helmsley, York, YO4 1NF
tel./fax. 01759 371 447

Confectionery Supplies [CS]
3 Lower Cathedral Road
Cardiff, Gwent
tel. 02920 372 161

Cooks Corner
50 Clayton Road,
Newcastle-upon-Tyne
NE1 4PF
tel. 0191 261 5481

Country Cutters [CC]
Lower Tresauldu
Dingestow, Monmouth
Gwent, NP5 4BQ
tel. 01600 740 448

Culpitt Cake Art, Culpitt Ltd
Jubilee Industrial Estate
Ashington, Northumberland,
NE63 8UQ
tel. 01670 814 545

Devon Ladye Products [DL]
Devon Ladye
The Studio, Coldharbour
Uffculme, Devon, EX15 3EE

Diane Harfield [DH]
Crickhollow, Berrington Drive
Bodenham, Hereford
HR1 3HT

F.M.M. [FMM]
Unit 5, Kings Park Ind. Estate
Primrose Hill, Kings Langley
Herts., WD4 8ST
tel. 01923 268 699
fax. 01923 261 226
clements@f-m-m.demon.co.uk

Great Impressions [GI]
14 Studley Drive, Swarland
Northumberland, NE65 9JT
tel./fax. 01670 787 061

Guy Paul & Co. Ltd
Unit B4, Foundry Way
Little End Road, Eaton Socon
Cambs. PE19 3JH

Hawthorn Hill [HH]
Unit 3, Milvale Studios,
Milvale Street, Middleport
Stoke-on-Trent, ST6 3NT
tel. 01782 811877

Holly Products [HP]
Holly Cottage, Hassall Green
Cheshire, CW11 4YA
tel./fax. 01270 761 403

Liberon (Super Woodglue)
Mountfield Ind. Estate,
Learoyd Road, New Romney,
Kent, TN28 8XU
tel. 01797 367 555

Orchard Products [OP]
51 Hallyburton Road
Hove, East Sussex, BN3 7GP
tel. 01273 419 418

Pierce Tandy Leather Craft
(leather punches)
Billing Park
Northampton, NN3 4BG

P.M.E. Sugarcraft [PME]
Brember Road, South Harrow
Middlesex, HA2 8UN
tel. 020 8864 0888
www.pmeltd.co.uk

Renshaw Scott Ltd
Crown Street
Liverpool, L8 7RF
tel. 0151 706 8200

W. Robertson (Billy's Blocks)
The Brambles, Ryton
Tyne and Wear, NE40 3AN
tel. 0191 413 8144

Squires Kitchen [SK]
Squires House
3 Waverley Lane
Farnham, Surrey, GU9 8BB
tel. 01252 711 749

Sugarflair (food colours)
Brunel Road
Manor Trading Estate
Benfleet, Essex, SS7 4PS
tel. 01268 752 891

The British Sugarcraft Guild
Wellington House
Messeter Place
Eltham, London, SE9 5DP
tel. 0208 859 6943

The Flower Basket (florists)
10 High Street
Much Wenlock, Shropshire
tel. 01952 728 101

The Old Bakery (Sunrise wires)
Kingston St Mary
Taunton, Somerset, TA2 8HW
tel. 01823 451205

The Porcelaina Society
46 Meadow Way, Tottington
Bury, Lancs., B18 3HU

The Secret Garden (florists)
Clayton Road, Jesmond
Tyne and Wear
tel. 0191 281 7753

Tinkertech Two [TT]
40 Langdon Road, Parkstone
Poole, Dorset, BH14 9EH
tel. 01202 738 049

Wilton [W]
Knightsbridge Bakeware
Centre (UK) Ltd
Chadwell Heath Lane
Romford, Essex RM6 4NP
tel. 020 8590 5959
www.cakedecoration.co.uk

Non-UK

Cakes & Co.
25 Rock Hill, Blackrock
Co. Dublin, Ireland
tel. + 353 1 283 6544

Cupid's Cake Decorations
2/90 Belford Street
Broadmeadow
NSW 2292, Australia
tel. +61 2 4962 1884

Cake Decorating School of Australia
Shop 7, Port Phillip Arcade
232 Flinders Street
Melbourne, VIC 3000
tel. +61 3 9654 5335

Beryl's Cake Decorating & Pastry Supplies
P.O. Box 1584, N. Springfield
VA22151-0584, USA
tel. + 1 800 488 2749

The European Cake Gallery
844 North Crowley Road,
Crowley, Texas 76036, USA
tel. + 817 297 2240

First published in 2001 by Merehurst, an imprint of Murdoch Books UK Ltd
Copyright© 2001 Murdoch Books UK Ltd
ISBN 1 85391 908 X

A catalogue record for this book is available from the British Library.
All rights reserved. No part of this publication may be reproduced, stored in a retrieval system, or transmitted in any form or by any means, electronic, mechanical, photocopying, recording or otherwise, without the prior written permission of the copyright owner.

Commissioning Editor:
Barbara Croxford
Designer:
Cathy Layzell
Project Editor:
Alastair Laing

CEO:
Robert Oerton
Publisher:
Catie Ziller
Publishing Manager:
Fia Fornari
Production Manager:
Lucy Byrne
Group General Manager:
Mark Smith
Group CEO/Publisher:
Anne Wilson

Photographer: Sue Atkinson
Templates: Chris King

Colour separation: Colourscan
Printed: Tien Wah Press in Singapore

Murdoch Books UK Ltd
Ferry House, 51–57 Lacy Road, Putney,
London, SW15 1PR
Tel: +44 (0)20 8355 1480
Fax: +44 (0)20 8355 1499
Murdoch Books UK Ltd is a subsidiary of Murdoch Magazines Pty Ltd.

Murdoch Books®
Wharf 8/9, 23 Hickson Road, Miller's Point,
NSW 2000, Australia
Tel: +61 (0)2 4352 7025
Fax: +61 (0)2 4352 7026
Murdoch Books® is a trademark of Murdoch Magazines Pty Ltd.

Other Merehurst sugarcraft titles:
Exotic Sugar Flowers for Cakes
Floral Wedding Cakes & Sprays
Sugar Skills: Garden Flowers in Sugar
Decorative Touches
Sugar Inspirations: Wild Flowers

HWLC LEARNING CENTRE